Simple Stock Trading Formulas

"How to Make Money Trading Stocks"

by Billy Williams

Disclaimer

It should not be assumed that the methods,
techniques, or
indicators presented in these products will be
profitable or will
not result in net losses. Past results are not
necessarily
indicative of future results. Examples
presented here are for
educational purposes only. These examples
are not
solicitations to buy or sell. The author,
publisher, and all
affiliates assume no responsibility for your
trading results.
There is a high risk in trading.

HYPOTHETICAL OR SIMULATED
PERFORMANCE RESULTS
HAVE CERTAIN INHERENT
LIMITATIONS. UNLIKE AN ACTUAL
PERFORMANCE RECORD, SIMULATED
RESULTS DO NOT
REPRESENT ACTUAL TRADING. ALSO,
SINCE THE TRADES
HAVE NOT ACTUALLY BEEN
EXECUTED, THE RESULTS MAY
HAVE UNDER- OR OVER-
COMPENSATED FOR THE IMPACT, IF
ANY, OF CERTAIN MARKET FACTORS,
SUCH AS LACK OF

What Others Are Saying

"Educated me tremendously! ...Everything was laid out in such a simple form that I was able to easily follow along. So far, I have profited over $300 in trades since starting this book. This may not seem like a lot but this is a great start considering I have never done this before." – Cassandra

"I have to say first that I know exactly zero about trading. I have been working on ways to generate income, and even though the market has been admittedly rough lately, I figured I could stand to learn something to be prepared when things started to pick up. This was a great place to start. The book is a logical step-by-step introduction to option trading. The author introduces key terms, and the in and out of trading. It is very thorough without getting mired in details. I certainly feel like I have a much better idea of what I could be doing financially to maximize my benefits. You can tell this is a very in depth approach (who ever said it superficial was reading another book, I think) by someone that certainly knows the subject." - Maege M.

"Overall it's a good lesson in how to review rank and buy stocks; its a great basic explanation of how to purchase options and how to assess stocks for option trading." – J. Crossland

"This is a very informative book. I never knew much about trading on the stock market, but this book is definitely a worthwhile resource. Before getting into how to buy, sell, and trade stocks, this book explains the terminology. Something that is extremely important if you wish to pursue

4

this venture. Once the terms have been explained, the author proceeds to talk about the different kinds of stocks available. I also like how this book tells you how to pick a stock to purchase and how you go about it. Basically this is Stock Trading 101 for people like me who know nothing about the stock market. Very easy to read and understand. A very good book and an invaluable resource." -McG

"I couldn't be more satisfied with this book. The author provides a professional and detailed approach to learning a solid foundation about option trading all provided by step-by-step methods and easy to understand writing. I decided to take a risk and buy this book when I saw that he had been published in the Future Magazine - I can now tell why because the content is amazing." – Manchester

"This is a no fluff book that gives you the hard facts about how to trade options successfully and a blueprint to do it. The book reinforces the basics to give you a strong foundation for option trading and actionable steps on how to apply them. Great addition to any beginner or veteran trader!" - Chris D.

Also by Billy Williams

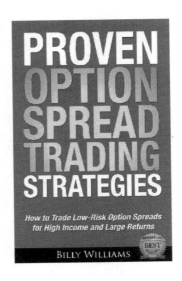

Proven Option Spread Trading Strategies

"How to Trade Low-Risk Option Spreads for High Income and Large Returns

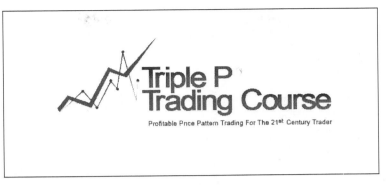

Triple P
Trading Course

Profitable Price Pattern Trading For The 21st Century Trader

To thank you for purchasing this book, I'd like to offer you a 47%+ loyalty discount on my **Triple P Trading Course** offered through Udemy.com.

You can access the discounted course homepage <u>by clicking here now</u>, or via the following link:

<u>https://www.udemy.com/triple-p-trading-course/?couponCode=winningthrusstf%21</u>

You can also use the coupon code "winningthrusstf!" at the course's homepage to receive your loyalty discount at <u>https://www.udemy.com/triple-p-trading-course/</u>.

Good Trading,

Billy Williams
www.stockoptionsystem.com

Table of Contents

1. Introduction

Every year, thousands, if not millions, of would-be stock trading millionaires come to the market armed with expensive trading systems and the latest indicators but quickly find out that they are unprepared for the volatility and brutality of the stock market.

Today, in the 21st century, the old rules like "buy and hold" don't seem to apply anymore. At any point in the current financial news cycle, you can learn of some new charge of corporate corruption, "cooking the books," conflicts of interest, Fed-created bubbles, insider trading, Ponzi schemes, fraud, moral hazards, debt crisis—and it just seems to keep getting worse.

In the end, who ends up getting hurt? Small investors like you.

But you probably already know that, just like you know you have to take more control of your investments than just relying on your fund manager or taking your financial advisor's advice.

Still, the question hangs in the air, "How do I go about making greater returns on my money without getting crushed?"

Fortunately, the answer is a lot simpler and easier than you might think, and I'll detail it for you in just a moment, but the first thing you need to understand is why the odds are stacked against you.

Every year, millions, if not billions, of dollars are spent on marketing programs to make you feel as whether you can't make money in the market without some expensive computer program or trading system or without turning your money over to some twenty-three-year-old recently graduated stock broker whose last job was at P.F. Chang's. As a result, you and a lot of other would-be traders are left confused and unsure about where to turn to for guidance.

That said, the first step to successful speculation in any market is having a deep-rooted understanding of price action.

By studying price action, you don't care about the latest product launch or debt restructuring a company announces, because all you care about is what the price of the stock is doing right now. You're not making predictions about where the company is going to be five or ten years from now, you're just looking to identify and exploit a stock's price action in the present.

And the results can be spectacular when you do it right.

Read any book in Jack Schwager's Market Wizard series, which profiles successful traders and you'll see that not only is it possible, but that everyday people are doing it every day. More importantly, none of these people are any smarter or have any advantages over you, other than the fact that they have found a method that matches their personality and that also exploits price movement in the market.

Fads go out of style, but the good ol' boring basics of price action never do. Why? The hopes and fears each individual brings to the market play out over and over again and are translated through price.

Fortunately, the art and science of price action isn't all that difficult to learn but without the basics, you can get into trouble.

But, after you have a sound foundation in the study and application of price action, you also need to have a formula that tells you when a move is underway.

In stock trading, professionals don't buy and sell stocks like the amateurs do who buy some stock on tip from their brother-in-law at the family BBQ or just randomly buy a stock because it's supposed to be a "good company".

Instead, the pros use a method that details a set of rules to tell them when a stock is setting up, when those setup conditions are met, and when to enter the stock's price move.

And that's what you'll find here in this book.

Here, you'll learn:

- The nature of the market and how to use it to profit.
- What stocks are and what is their purpose?
- Why volatility frightens the majority of traders but how you can profit from it.
- The dual relationship of price and volume.

- What roles do stock exchanges play?
- What key indicators to use to signal when to get into the market (and when to stay out).
- The best price patterns to trade for consistent winners.
- How to spot market reversals and how to profit from them.
- What warning signs to watch for so that you don't get wiped out financially.
- What 3 indicators to combine to form an unbeatable winning formula for trading.
- What Big Daddy is and how to use it to always be on the right side of the trend.
- The only two types of price action there are in the market and how to use them for winning trades over and over again.
- How to spot turns in the market and how to use them to time your entries (and exits).
- 7 trading formulas to help you find winning trades in any market environment.
- Both fundamental and technical formulas to help you rack up above-average returns.
- And much, much more.

More than skill building and education, you're going to learn a set of reliable trading formulas that have a vast application to trading.

Start now and begin reading about the history of the market and its role in the global economy which will help you understand how the game operates. Later, you'll learn how to read "under the hood" and how to spot superior, well-oiled companies that have durable competitive advantages in their marketplace which keep cranking out profits. Knowing how to spot these companies provides you a fertile field of trading opportunities.

If you want to jump ahead and start learning about price action, technical analysis, and the trading formulas themselves, then skip ahead to Chapter 7 and go from there.

In the final chapter, you'll see detailed real-life examples of how all the tools in this book come together and form a powerful method for extracting profits from the stock market that is both evergreen and timeless.

The tools and methods here will serve you for a long time if you take the time to master them, so get started now.

14

Good Trading,

Billy Williams
www.stockoptionsystem.com

2. Stock Basics

This chapter will look at what it really means to "own" a stock and reflect on why the modern definition of "ownership" is so constrained and nebulous. In the process, it will cover important issues in corporate governance.

When you need money to purchase something you currently cannot afford, such as a car, house, or new appliance, you can go to a bank and take out a loan. In return for receiving a loan from the bank, you agree to make an interest payment every few months until you have paid the loan off in full. When a company needs to purchase something it cannot afford, such as a new factory or piece of equipment, it has the additional option of bypassing banks and going directly to investors who have extra money they would like to earn a return on.

There are two ways an agreement between a company and its investors can be structured so that each party gets what it wants. The first option is a bond. A bond is similar to a bank loan in that the company agrees to pay the investors an interest payment every period (usually every six months) and then to repay the original loan amount in full at the end of the bond's term. The second option is to issue stock.

Issuing stock involves selling partial ownership of the company to investors. If the company is successful in its investments, it will earn additional profits in the future. After investing a portion of these profits back into the business to build even more factories or buy even more equipment, the company may split the remaining earnings among all the owners, in equal proportion to the percentage of the company each investor owns.

A key difference between stocks and bonds for investors is the risk/reward equation. With a bond, the investors' upside is limited—the best they can do is receive fixed interest payments and get their money back at the end of the term. With a stock, the upside is unlimited, because they can share in the profit growth of the company.

The company's view, of course, is precisely the opposite. For a company, issuing stock may be a more flexible and less risky source of funding if it is planning a project that may have uncertain results. If a project is unsuccessful and a company has taken out loans (or bonds) to finance it, the company may not have enough cash to pay back its loans. It may have to declare bankruptcy and in effect be taken over by its creditors (the purchasers of the bonds). On the other hand, if the company issues stock to finance the project, it can just stop paying any dividends for a few years. This is very important. Bond holders expect to get their money back from a loan on a fixed schedule, but stockholders accept the chance of losses in exchange for the potential for higher returns. This makes stocks more risky for investors than bonds, but less risky for the company issuing them.

So if I am an owner of McDonald's, why do I still have to pay for hamburgers?

It is important to understand just what owning shares of a company like McDonald's means. Ownership is not an altogether clear concept in the modern economic system. While it is true that owning shares of a stock like McDonald's does mean that you own part of the company, your rights and privileges as an "owner" are pretty much limited to collecting dividend checks. There are a few good reasons for this:

1. The amount of the company that you own will likely be miniscule. Say McDonald's has 1 billion shares outstanding as of its last reporting quarter. If you own 100 shares, then you own one ten-millionth of the company. Not quite

enough of a stake for employees at the cash registers to remember your name.

2. There will be hundreds of thousands of other "owners" like you who will invariably have different ideas about how the business should be run. It would be a massive coordination problem to involve everyone in any kind of business decision.

3. Many of the "owners" know nothing about the fast-food business. It would not make sense to channel business decisions through them.

On the surface, this presents a bit of a problem. If the owners of the company are not fit to manage it, then who is? The solution devised by the markets is to hire a professional management team to run the company for the ostensible benefit of the shareholders. So technically, if you own a share of McDonald's, the CEO and the rest of the management team work on your behalf to make sure the company generates as much profit as possible, thereby maximizing your future dividends.

Of course, this does not really solve the problem of coordinating among owners, since someone must still choose who the management team will be. Even agreeing on who to hire for a management team would be a nearly impossible coordination and knowledge problem for the hundreds of thousands of McDonald's shareholders to solve. The solution is a smaller 5-15 person Board of Directors that is responsible for representing the shareholders of the company by overseeing the selection and ongoing monitoring of the management team. Board members are bound by what is called a fiduciary duty to shareholders. This means that they are legally obligated to look out for the best interests of shareholders over their own best interests.

In reality, of course, the coordination and knowledge problems of having multiple owners are not so easily solved. The "oversight" problem never really goes away, no matter how many levels you take it to. Even agreeing on a board to oversee the management team that oversees the business is problematic. Technically, shareholders appoint board members by a majority vote. But shareholders come from all across the country and the world, and there is no way they could agree on a common set of people they trust to represent their interests. The result is that board members are often appointed to their roles by the management team—the same team they are supposed to supervise! In some cases, they may even be the CEO's golfing buddies!

The conflict of interest here should be obvious—in many cases, the CEO gets to hire his or her own bosses.

Disgruntled shareholders do have some options for trying to "take back" a company from a management team they feel is holding it hostage or taking too much of its value for themselves. Companies are required to have an annual shareholder meeting during which shareholders can vote on different measures and express their general grievances.

But most decision-making still happens through the board. To really take control of a company, shareholders would need to get their own candidates onto the board. This can be difficult. While companies are required to hold some kind of election for the board members, in most cases this is just a "Soviet-style" up/down vote with only one person running! Sometimes very large shareholders are able to nominate candidates to run against the management's choices, but winning what is called "proxy fights" can be quite difficult and expensive. Dissident shareholders attempting to win a hostile proxy fight must contact all the other shareholders of the company and convince them to vote against the management's choices and for their own choices. Most shareholders find this too difficult and expensive to manage. Instead, they prefer to just sell their shares to someone else if they are unhappy with a company's direction.

The potential conflict of interest between management and shareholders is actually a pretty serious and fundamental issue with modern capitalism. Before the days of the contemporary stock market, most companies were owned and operated by the same person or family. This resulted in very clear incentives for the manager, since it was his or her money that could be lost. While the fractional share ownership system has many advantages in terms of capital allocation (more on this later), it also has very real costs. One of these is the cost for investors to monitor the management team. This is one of the primary functions that active investment managers serve in the economy.

What good is being an owner if I can't tell anyone what to do?

The reason to own stocks for the long-term is to collect dividend payments in the future. When a company makes a profit, it will usually distribute a portion of the money to its shareholders in what is called a dividend. These payments can occur on a quarterly or annual basis. If you own a stock for a long time and the company does well, the value you get in dividends over your lifetime may dramatically exceed the price you originally paid for the stock.

In the short-term, of course, you may also be able to make a profit by selling your shares to someone else for a higher price than you bought them for. It is the price that these secondary exchanges of shares take place at that is reported in the newspaper every day. But if the buyers in these transactions are rational, they will not be willing to pay more money than they think the dividends will be worth in the future. We will talk more about the process of buying and selling shares of a stock on a secondary exchange like the New York Stock Exchange in the next chapter.

3. House of Finance: the Stock Exchange

This chapter will look at what actually goes on in a contemporary stock exchange, putting into concrete terms what "buying a stock" really means.

To buy a share of a stock, you first must have an account with a company called a "brokerage" that has the technology and relationships necessary to trade stocks. In the old days, this brokerage would employ actual people ("stock brokers") that you could call on the phone and manually give your order to. These brokers may also have actively called you with stock tips or general financial advice. This kind of model is now known as a "full-service" brokerage, and it still exists at firms like Morgan Stanley.

A newer model is the online-only discount brokerage, utilized by companies such as E*TRADE and Ameritrade. Discount brokerages operate more of a "self-serve" model in that they leave the customer responsible for order entry via a website, and they usually do not offer any guidance or advice from an investment professional. However, discount brokerages usually charge much lower fees for each trade than full-service brokerages do.

Whether your order is entered manually via your discount brokerage's website or relayed verbally to a full-service broker, the next step is the same. Your broker sends your order to an exchange like the New York Stock Exchange.

What Really Happens at the Stock Exchange

The nature of what actually happens at a stock exchange has changed a lot over the past twenty years. The largest and most famous stock exchange in the United States is the New York Stock Exchange (NYSE). For most of its history, trading at the NYSE took place between human beings on an actual "exchange floor" located in downtown Manhattan. Each brokerage firm would have to buy a "seat" at the stock exchange, which would entitle it to have its own traders or clerks present on the floor. When a customer issued an order to buy or sell shares, the firm would relay the instructions to its representative on the floor, who would be responsible for executing it or finding another trader to execute it.

To avoid having a complete madhouse, there were set "stations" of the floor devoted to trading particular stocks.

At these stations a special trader known as a "specialist" would reside. The specialist's job was to facilitate an orderly market for his stock or stocks, essentially matching buyers and sellers by running a continuous auction. Traders who wanted to buy or sell stocks would tell the specialist, who would match them with the person offering the best price on the other side of the trade, i.e., the person willing to offer the highest price if you were buying or the lowest price if you were selling. In situations where there were not enough buyers or sellers present to find a match, the specialist could also buy or sell shares out of his or her own inventory by acting as a "market maker."

Today, most trading occurs electronically rather than on a physical exchange floor. Once you enter your order, it is automatically transferred to the exchange via your brokerage's computer systems. The order process works much like the floor, except instead of a specialist standing at a physical location and keeping track of who is willing to buy or sell and at what prices a computer database simply records the information and automatically matches buyers and sellers.

To visualize how this happens, we need to add one more piece to the puzzle. When you enter your order with your broker, you have a choice of how you want it to be executed. You can use a "market order," which tells your broker you want to execute the order immediately at the best price available, or you can use a "limit order," which tells your broker you only want to buy or sell at a particular price. For instance, if you want to buy McDonald's shares and use a limit order with a price of $20 a share, your order will only be executed if someone is willing to sell those shares to you for $20 or less. The database (or specialist) keeps a record of all these limit orders arranged by price, as in the table below.

Bids (Buy Orders)	Asks (Sell Orders)
$19.99 x 300	$20.01 x 100
$19.97 x 1,000	$20.03 x 500
$19.95 x 200	$20.05 x 1,000
$19.90 x 300	$20.07 x 400

Suppose someone in the market above entered an order to "sell 300 shares at market." The trade would immediately be executed at the price of the highest bid (buy offer) for 300 shares, or $19.99 a share. If someone entered an order to "sell 1300 shares a market," 300 of those shares would be sold at $19.99 and 1,000 would be sold at $19.97.

With electronic exchanges, there is no "person" designated to keep track of the orders and ensure an orderly market. However, there are electronic market-making firms that make money by ensuring a liquid market. Market makers in an electronic sense are simply traders who are willing to both buy and sell large amounts of a stock at the same time. For instance, a market maker might be willing to buy up to 5,000 shares of McDonald's at $19.99 and sell up to 5,000 shares of McDonald's at $20.01. By doing this, the market maker can capture the two-cent spread between the prices they are buying and selling at. If in one minute someone comes in and buys 500 shares at market, and in the next minute another person sells 500 shares at market, the market maker can pocket 500 x 2 cents = $10 for providing this liquidity.

The usefulness of stock exchanges

To see why stock exchanges are useful, imagine what the process of buying a stock like McDonald's would be like without them. Stocks do not just appear out of nowhere—you would have to find someone that already owns the shares and is willing to sell them to you in order to complete the purchase. This would not be easy in itself. Suppose you were lucky enough to find that your neighbor owned shares you were interested in buying and was considering selling them. Even then you would still not know the fair price to buy the shares from him for. And how would you know there is not someone else in a town a few miles away that might be willing to sell you the same shares for less money?

Put in another way, though stock prices seem to appear magically out of the pages of the newspaper or the Yahoo! Finance section every day, every quote coming across the ticker actually represents a real exchange of shares for money between two consenting investors or traders. The "prices" reported are simply the prevailing prices at which these exchanges are taking place. Without stock exchanges, there would be huge costs involved with buying or selling a share, since you would have to search far and wide for the person on the other side of the trade who would give you the best price. The stock exchange provides a central place for everyone in the market to buy or sell shares with the confidence that they are always getting the best price because everyone else is there, too.

4. Efficient Market Theory & Thinking For Yourself

This chapter will look at the logic of the Efficient Market Hypothesis, analyze the evidence for and against it, and argue that understanding its logic is essential for individual investors even if it is not entirely correct.

If you have been following the text closely, you might be feeling understandably upset about the number of contingencies so far. To review, some of these include:

• A stock with an intrinsic value that is lower than its share price is a screaming buy, but intrinsic value is highly sensitive to assumptions about the time value of money.

• It is possible to estimate the time value of money from treasury yields, but the market risk premium—the amount of extra compensation investors demand to hold risky assets—can vary unpredictably.

• Ratios like the P/E, P/S, and P/B can be great "rule of thumb" shortcuts for finding cheap stocks, but stocks might be justifiably cheap due to slow growth, low ROE, or a deteriorating balance sheet.

There is actually a good reason why we have to be extremely careful and ask the "buts" and why we have to be extremely cautious of anything that seems "too good to be true" in the investing world. That reason is the Efficient Market Hypothesis.

The Efficient Market Hypothesis (EMH) was formally developed in the 1960s at the University of Chicago. It has different forms, but generally asserts that stock prices already incorporate all known information. A corollary to this is that an individual investor can only outperform the overall stock market as a result of getting lucky (correctly guessing by random chance which companies will have unexpectedly positive news in the future), taking on more risk (assets that may fluctuate wildly in price should return more than more stable assets over the long-term in an efficient market, since investors will demand a premium return in order to be compensated for the risk), or possessing inside information.

Whether EMH actually holds or not is subject to fierce debate, which we will delve into a bit below, but it is essential for even the most ardent anti-EMHer to understand its underlying logic before trying to pick any individual stocks. The logic of EMH basically comes down to the fact that risk-free profits should not exist. To see why, imagine that there are two different assets that are expected to produce similar cash flows for investors in the future. If one asset is trading at $98 a share while the other is at $100 a share, it would make sense to sell the one at $98 and buy the one at $100. But if enough people started doing this, the prices would quickly converge because everyone would want to sell the overpriced asset and sell the underpriced asset until this was the case. The "supply" of sellers of the first asset at $98 a share would disappear, as would the supply of buyers of the second asset at $101.

In the stock market today, most trades take place between professional investors such as hedge fund managers, mutual fund managers, and professional traders. These investors are highly motivated to do thorough research and analysis on the companies they are buying. Thus, there is reason to think that obvious pricing discrepancies like the one above would ever be allowed to exist. This is known as the "no arbitrage" condition and in its extreme case it means that all stocks are "rationally" priced and that there is no way to make excess profits in the stock market.

Under the EMH, what drives market volatility (movement in share prices) is news. Any time there is new information that is released to the market, that information results in a nearly instantaneous adjustment of share prices, as you would expect from the theory of intrinsic value, in order to incorporate the news. But under EMH, mis-pricings (divergence between intrinsic value and market price) are fleeting in nature.

Supporting Evidence from Mutual Fund Returns

One prediction of EMH is that it would be nearly impossible to earn returns above the market without taking on more risk than the market.

Extensive research on mutual fund returns has confirmed that professional investors fail to beat a passive index of all stocks over time:

• In the five-year period ending on Dec 31, 2012, Standard and Poor's estimates that 62% of all US large cap equity funds were outperformed by the passive S&P 500 benchmark.

• Academic surveys of research done over the past twenty years have shown that actively managed funds as a whole

33

underperform the stock market by a level equal to their fees, implying that the average investor would have been much better off with a low-cost index fund or ETF.

However, this does not necessarily imply an efficient market. In fact, in a world where all equity trades take place between professional investors, it would be nearly impossible for active investors as a whole to "beat" passive investors, since it would be active investors who would determine stock prices.

A better measure of market efficiency might be whether "smart" investors can reliably beat the market—something that EMH would prevent if true (this is distinct from investors beating the market due to luck; there will always be some investors who outperform the market due to random chance). The evidence is somewhat mixed on this point, but again is generally tilted toward the efficient market argument. Most studies indicate that past performance is a poor measure of future long-term performance. In other words, buying the mutual funds that have performed the best in the past would not be a profitable long-term strategy. This would seem to indicate that those mutual funds' past performance was a result of luck rather than any "skill" in identifying mispriced stocks.

Of course, there is strong anecdotal evidence that some investors do manage to repeatedly perform better than the market averages. Famous investors like Warren Buffett, George Soros, and other top hedge-fund managers have seemed to beat the odds, with levels of past success that would be very unlikely to occur in a purely random world. Indeed, some studies by famous financial economists have lent weight to these anecdotal observations by indicating that the top 2% of managers do seem to be capable of consistently producing alpha. However, in many cases the strategies these managers run are off limits to the individual investor, and fees may still capture most of the outperformance.

Counter-evidence from factor returns

While data from mutual-fund returns seems mostly to support a weak form of the EMH, several well-known anomalies, or deviations from the expected behavior, complicate the picture.

Three generally accepted "anomalies" of EMH (many more are less widely accepted) are the size effect, the valuation effect, and the momentum effect.

Research on the size effect shows that companies with smaller market capitalizations have historically outperformed those with large market capitalizations, even after controlling for their higher risk. Research conducted by Eugene Fama and Kenneth French shows that stocks with market capitalizations in the smallest 30% of companies in the data set outperformed those with market caps in the largest 30% by an average of 4.5% a year since 1926, when the data set begins. Small stocks had an average annualized return of 15.4% vs. 10.8% for large stocks. While quite impressive, this outperformance was volatile, as the chart below shows that there were many five-year periods when large stocks actually outperformed small stocks. In fact, while small stocks outperformed impressively overall, they did so in only 49% of all individual months.

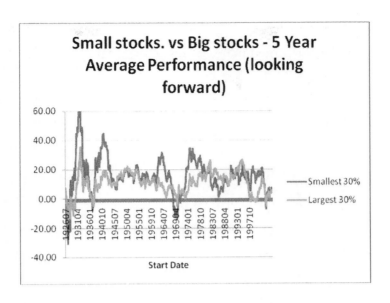

Research on the valuation effect shows that companies with low price/book (P/B) multiples have historically outperformed those with higher P/B multiples. Again using research from Kenneth French's Dartmouth website, a portfolio that bought the lowest 30% of stocks by the p/b ratio every year and held them for a year would have returned an average of nearly 18% a year, versus only 12% for an equally weighted portfolio of stocks with an average multiple. This is quite significant outperformance. Again, this outperformance did not persist over every time period.

Research on the momentum effect shows that companies that have performed the best over the past six months to one year tend to perform better than the set of companies that have performed the worst over a similar period.

Of course, the EMH implies that as soon as an anomaly becomes popularized, it will likely cease to exist. This can be seen in an example. Imagine that stocks always went up on Fridays and down on Mondays. If this anomaly became widely known, many would try to buy stocks on Thursday afternoon right before the close and sell them at a similar time on Friday afternoon in order to capture this Friday bounce. But if everyone tried to buy shares on Thursday afternoon and sell on Friday afternoon, by simple supply and demand, prices would have to go up on Thursday and down on Friday. The Friday boom would turn into a Friday bust.

Investors who try to take advantage of any proclaimed anomaly must be very aware of the potential for this dynamic to show up again and again. As soon as it appears that "easy money" is on the table, thousands of aggressively return-seeking fund managers will immediately try to grab it.

Implications for Individual Investors

While the degree to which stock prices are efficient remains a subject of debate, the evidence from investor returns shows that for the majority of individual investors, they might as well be. Market efficiency has some sobering lessons for aspiring stock-pickers who remain unconvinced of its full validity:

• If something seems like "easy money," pause. Remember that thousands of other professional investors have observed the same facts as you and decided to pass. Ask yourself what you could be missing.

• Always approach an investment by first understanding why the stock is trading like it is. Only then consider whether you think the market is right or wrong. For instance, do not buy a stock that is selling at a discount to its industry on a number of metrics just because it looks cheap. First understand why that stock may be cheap, then develop your own view on whether the valuation is justified or not.

• Remember that there is always someone else "on the other side of the trade." Could this person be more informed than you or know something you do not? What do you know or realize that the person selling the stock to you is missing?

4.1. News & Its Context

This chapter will look at the market's real focus on a day-to-day basis—news. We will start by looking at the importance of earnings announcements, including how hedge funds have turned investing into a quarterly earnings prediction game and how individual investors should play this game. Finally, we will look at momentum investors and again examine the impact on individual investors.

You may recall from the previous chapter that the Efficient Market Hypothesis predicts that it is news events that drive stock prices. In other words, stock prices nearly instantaneously react to new information entering the market.

Some of the biggest news events that drive the prices of individual stocks are earnings announcements. In the US, companies announce their financial results every three months. Prior to the announcement, Wall Street analysts feverishly work on building their own predictions called "earnings estimates." The average of these predictions is known as the "consensus earnings estimate" and is generally thought to be built into the stock price (in other words, this is what the market expects). Companies that outperform the consensus earnings estimate usually see their stock price go up, while those that fall below the consensus surprise the market in a negative way and generally see their stock price go down.

For many hedge funds, investing has essentially become an earnings prediction game. These professional investors try to predict the direction of a company's earnings announcements better than anyone else, knowing that if they are right, the market will move in their direction after the announcement. Of course, with so many analysts trying to outguess the market, outguessing the market actually becomes progressively harder and harder. One of the things that makes it so hard is the fact that the market's expectations are not always obvious. Sometimes if enough hedge funds are expecting an announcement far above the Wall Street consensus earnings estimate, a stock will actually go down if it only narrowly beats the consensus number. Of course, hedge funds do not tell the market what they are expecting, so it can be hard to guess exactly how a stock will react.

To predict earnings, Wall Street analysts use several techniques:

1. Most analysts start with an in-depth financial model in Microsoft Excel. This model will usually contain every line item of a company's financial statements over the past five to ten years.

2. An analyst will develop his or her own views of how things will look in the future through a combination of extrapolating past trends, looking at how similar companies have been doing, and talking extensively with company management in order to gain an edge in understanding the business.

3. To refine these models, the analyst will likely conduct "channel checks" by calling on the distributors of a company's products to see how well they are selling and talking to competitors to gauge how the pricing in an industry is holding up.

Some observers have cautioned that this kind of high-stakes earnings-game investing makes it very tempting to use inside information. It is illegal in the United States to trade stocks based on non-public knowledge of a company's earnings (this would include things like being tipped off by a member of the management team before a company announces). In the past couple years, several high-profile hedge funds have run afoul of these regulations and gotten into trouble with the Securities and Exchange Commission (SEC).

Use the earnings game to your advantage

It is generally difficult for the individual investor to successfully compete in the earnings prediction game. Wall Street analysts have too many informational advantages. One key to successful stock-picking at the individual level is to compete indirectly with Wall Street. In other words, do not try to beat them at their own game, but be strategic and take advantage of their weaknesses instead. For instance, if you have a positive long-term view of a company and are looking to get into the stock for the long term, you may want to use a temporary fall in the price of the shares after an earnings miss as an opportunity to buy in at a low price. Just make sure that nothing in the earnings announcement has changed your favorable long-term view.

Momentum

Another class of investors is not particularly concerned with either intrinsic value or earnings, but instead focused purely on the stock price and which direction it is heading in.

Momentum-driven investors are frequently looked down on by fundamental analysts, who see them as "dumb" money. But as we saw in the last chapter, there is pretty strong evidence that buying past winners and selling past losers is a profitable strategy over the long term. There are a few fundamental reasons stock prices might not be totally random, but instead tend to "trend" at important times:

• It can take a long time for large institutional investors like mutual funds and pension funds to enter into positions in a stock. This is because they are managing so much money that they need to space out the time period in which they buy a new stock in order not to flood the market with "buy" orders and make the price go up.

• Professional investors tend to "herd" together for various reasons (either they are directly sharing ideas, or it is just the professionally safe path to take, because if the stock you buy goes down, at least you can claim that plenty of other people made the same mistake). Once one big fund accumulates a position, pushing the price up in the process, others are likely to follow.

44

• New information may not be instantaneously incorporated into the stock price. If, for instance, a company's new products are selling far better than anyone expected, different analysts may figure this out at different times. This can create sustained buying pressure on a stock.

• Somebody may have non-public information. The first buyers in a trend may be analysts with inside information, or company insiders that know something is up. These first buyers cause the stock price to go up initially. Once the news travels, the price continues to go up until the information is completely reflected.

• Once a stock has gone up a lot (for any reason), momentum investors will flood in and purchase its shares, pushing it up even more. In this sense, momentum can be a self-fulfilling phenomenon (the mere fact that a lot of people think it exists actually makes it exist).

It is important to note that these factors fall into two categories: some are fundamental factors related to the transmission of information. Others are technical factors related only to the short-term supply and demand for shares of a company's stock. Often, both of these factors are involved. A stock's momentum run can start on the back of fundamental factors, such as a pick-up in the company's business that the market does not instantaneously recognize, but then continue after favorable news has already been fully priced in because of technical factors.

Be careful when "fighting the tape"

Long-time stock traders like to say that it is never a good idea to "fight the tape." In other words, if the market seems intent on sending the price of a company's shares down, it is not a good idea to go against the grain and buy them. This may generally be sage advice, but it is confusing to many, as it goes against the "buy low, sell high" value investing ethos favored by famous investors like Warren Buffett.

A more nuanced view would be "don't fight the tape unless you have a good reason." There is usually a reason why stock prices react the way they do. If you believe that reason has become obvious and that the market has moved past the "fundamental" momentum stage and into the "technical" one, then buying a stock that has gotten beaten down to below its fair value can be a very profitable strategy. But make sure that you really understand the business and have a good reason for thinking that it will be worth more in the long term than it is today. This is why Buffett only owns a small and concentrated portfolio of companies with relatively simple businesses that he can understand.

"Fighting the tape" can be really dangerous because there is always a strong chance that somebody who is selling knows something that you do not. They might even be aware of non-public information. For most individual investors who do not have the time to really understand a business in as much detail as professional investors like Warren Buffett, it is probably better to wait for a stock price to stabilize for a couple months before rushing in and buying (e.g., look for a chart that has flattened out and is no longer jailing).

On the other hand, buying stocks that have already gone up in price can be difficult because it feels like you may have already "missed out on the party." But this can actually be a profitable strategy over the long term. A key to investing in these kinds of momentum stocks is to get out (sell) once it seems like the positive business news has been more than priced in and the only buyers remaining are momentum chasers. Evidence of this might be when the P/E ratio of the stock has reached unjustifiable levels and the stock is frequently mentioned in the financial news. Stocks that are relying on technical momentum factors can break and fall *sharply for little reason, since even a small fall will cause the whole momentum crowd to bail out of their positions en masse. Netflix (NFLX) is a great example of this in recent times.*

5. Understanding Stock Value & Opportunity

The objective of any long-term investor is to purchase a stock for less money than it is truly "worth." This chapter will take up the topic of what the long-term worth of a stock really is. It will reiterate why the value of a stock comes from its dividends, explain how you can determine the present value of future dividends using something called the time value of money, and wrap up by talking about the market risk premium.

As we saw in the last chapter, in the short term, stock prices merely reflect the prevailing price that stocks change hands at on major secondary exchanges. This price, in turn, reflects the supply and demand for shares of that company. If there is a change in one of these variables, then the price will adjust in order to clear the market (equal number of buyers and sellers). For instance, if the supply of shares on the secondary market goes up because the economy has entered a recession and many people need to sell their investments to raise cash and pay off their bills, then the price will have to adjust downward in order to entice more buyers to step in and clear the market (supply always has to meet demand).

In the long term, what drives "demand" for a stock are expectations about the future value of a company's dividends. Remember from the last chapter that in a totally rational world, receiving dividends in the future is the only reason to own shares, since an investment is only valuable if it will give you cash in the future. Taking this a step further, in a rational world, the price you should be willing to pay for a share of stock is the current value of its future dividend stream. This is known as a stock's intrinsic value. You can think of it as the value that a person who planned to hold a stock literally forever would receive as a result of cashing dividend checks. But this, of course, brings up a number of questions. How do we calculate the current value of future payments? And how do we even know how many dividends the company will pay in the future?

We will discuss the first of these questions below and leave the second for the next chapter.

The time value of money

The concept of a time value of money might seem a bit strange, since it seems like $1 should always be worth $1 pretty much by definition, but given the choice between receiving $1 now and $1 five years from now, most people would rationally prefer to receive the $1 now. There are different levels of reasons for this. At one level, $1 today will probably buy you more things than $1 five years from now because of inflation. For instance, a pound of bread cost $.20 in 1980 but $1.10 in 2010, so in bread terms a dollar in 1980 was worth five times a dollar in 2010. At another level, if you had $1 today, you could do something with it, like invest it. Even if you put it in an ultra-safe investment like a CD (certificate of deposit), you could get back more than $1 five years from now.

So how much is $1 five years from now worth today? One way to think about this is to extend the example from above and imagine having to choose between a smaller amount of money today versus a larger amount five years from now. Offered a choice between ten cents today or $1 five years from now, most people would take the $1 five years from now. You would have to get a great rate of return on a ten-cent investment today to get $1 five years from now. There will be some point though, be it 75 cents, 80 cents, or maybe even 90 cents, where you would be indifferent between receiving the smaller amount of money today and $1 five years from now. The amount where there is indifference is precisely the amount we mean when we ask what $1 five years from now is worth. In other words, if you are indifferent about receiving 80 cents today or $1 five years from now, then $1 five years from now must be worth 80 cents to you today. If we can find the value of $1 five years from now in this way, then there is no reason we cannot also assign a value of $1 at any point in the future— one, three, seven, ten, thirteen years into the future. This is precisely what we need to do to find the current value of an expected stream of dividends from a stock.

When evaluating a potential investment, we can estimate the time value of money by looking at the returns we can get on holding an alternative risk-free asset like a government treasury bond. Imagine that we are evaluating the value of a stock that is expected to pay a single dividend of $100 ten years from now and then go bankrupt (this, of course, is not a realistic example, but is useful for illustrative purposes). To determine what price we should be willing to pay for the stock today, we can start by looking at the price of a zero-coon US Treasury bond. A zero-coon treasury bond is effectively a loan to the US government for ten years. At the end of the loan, the government guarantees that they will pay us back $100. If a 10-year $100 zero-coon bond is currently selling for $80 (meaning you can pay $80 today to get back $100 ten years from now), then we should not be willing to pay more than $80 for the stock. Why? Because if the stock cost more than that, we could just invest in the treasury bond instead and achieve the same outcome for less money.

In fact, if the stock is risky, we may be willing to pay significantly less than $80. This is because with all things being equal, we would much rather own the risk-free bond than a stock where there is a significant chance that we may not be paid back anything at all.

The "Market Risk Premium"

The flipside of the idea that we should be willing to pay more money for a risk-free bond than a risky stock is saying that over time and on average, we should expect risky stocks to return more than risky bonds. To see why, consider the example above. Though a zero-coon bond and our hypothetical dividend-paying stock are both expected to give us $100 ten years from now, we might be able to buy the stock at $60 and the bond at $80. If everything goes as expected, the return on the bond would be 100/80, or 25% on our initial investment. With the stock, we would get a

100/60 or 67% return on our initial investment. On an annualized basis (calculating percentage return per year), this works out to a 5.2% annual return on the stock and a 2.3% annual return on the bond. The difference between the returns of stocks and bonds—about 3% a year in this example—is known as the "market risk premium." This is the additional expected return that investors demand in order to hold stocks instead of risk-free bonds.

One of the things that makes determining the fair "intrinsic value" of a stock so difficult is that even if you were able to perfectly predict future dividends (which, as we shall see in the next chapter, is quite a stretch), the fair value of stocks could still vary widely if the market-risk premium changes. This can be the case in significant bear-market recessions, like the one in 2008 when there was a sudden loss in appetite to take risk. In this kind of environment, investors may shift from demanding a premium of 1% or 2% a year in order to feel comfortable holding stocks to demanding a premium of 5% or 6%. This can have an enormous impact on stock prices, even if there are no fundamental changes in the long-term prospects of the underlying businesses at all.

The market-risk premium for US stocks is generally estimated to be around 6% per year, meaning that in the past stocks returned 6% more than bonds. However, the risk premium can vary considerably from year to year and decade to decade. Some experts estimate that the forward-looking risk premium (which is what really counts) may be only 3% or 4% today. One way to estimate the forward-looking risk premium (the amount that stocks can be expected to outperform bonds over the long term) is to estimate the future returns of stocks and compare this to the 30 Yr Treasury Yield (the return you would get from holding a thirty-year US Government bond until maturity). The future return for stocks can be estimated as the dividend yield plus the growth rate in dividends plus any expected change in the dividend yield (the latter accounts for a change in stock market valuation). Using the dividend growth rate over the past twenty years of roughly 4% and a current dividend yield of 2.1%, this would mean that you could expect stocks to return roughly 6% a year over the next ten years or so. By comparing this to a ten-year treasury rate of 2% and a thirty-year rate of around 3%, we could estimate the current risk premium at between 3% and 4% a year.

5.1. Price Ratios & Stock Leadership

Uncovering Diamonds with DCF Analysis

This chapter will look at several "rule of thumb" approaches to stock market valuation that involve ratios. These are less sensitive to assumptions than a pure DCF approach.

The discounted cash flow models we described in the previous chapter have two big advantages. First, they are the theoretically correct way to value a stock, so if you apply the "correct" assumptions, you will get a theoretically "correct" stock price down to the decimal point. Second, and more importantly, the process of going through the DCF exercise tends to teach you a lot about the business you are analyzing and how it operates. However, as we pointed out, the big problem with a DCF analysis is that is incredibly sensitive to changes in assumptions, particularly the long-term growth rate of revenues and the discount rate/time value of the money you are using (which we did not even get into in detail). And it is almost impossible to know which assumptions are "correct."

Thankfully, there is an alternative to this kind of analysis. For a quicker way to see if a stock price looks "cheap" or "expensive" relative to its intrinsic value, analysts use various ratios of a company's stock price to the fundamental performance of its underlying businesses. The most common of these is the price to earnings ratio, or PE (commonly said "P" to "E," "PE Multiple," or just "Multiple"). To calculate this important ratio, simply find the price per share of a stock and divide it by its earnings per share (which you can find from the bottom line of the income statement or from just about any financial website). This ratio is of limited use on its own, but it can be very useful when compared to:

1. The average multiple the company has traded at in its past

2. The average multiple for stocks in the overall market

3. The average multiple for companies in its industry.

Comparing the PE multiple of a company to its competitors, the overall market, and its own history can give you a sense of whether the shares look "cheap" or "expensive" (lower is better). Best of all, this "rule of thumb" approach does not rely on many assumptions at all. Once you have more experience analyzing stocks you will develop an intuitive feel for what kind of multiple a company "should" be trading at based on a host of other factors we will go through in the next few chapters.

The logic of the PE ratio is pretty simple. What you are paying for when you buy a stock is really its earnings. Of course, it is the dividends that make a stock valuable in the long term. But if you trust management (and this can be a big if—we will get into this later), then you have to think that they are going to reinvest whatever earnings they do not give back to shareholders into the business in order to grow dividends even more in the future. Since price is what you are paying for when you buy a stock and earnings are a measure of what you are getting, the price to earnings ratio makes good sense as a measure of "value" (what you are paying relative to what you are getting). Over the past fifty years, the average P/E of the overall stock market has fluctuated between about 8 and 30, with the average around 15.

58

In using multiples, you are in effect piggybacking on the work of the market. It's like saying "I know I should do this complicated DCF analysis to determine what price I should be willing to pay for these shares, but I already know how much money the company is making, and I know how the market is valuing similar companies in its industry as well as how it has valued this company in the past. Why don't I use that information instead of making a bunch of wild guesses about future growth rates?"

Other ratios: P/S, P/R, Div Yield, FCF Yield

While the "P to E" is the most common ratio because of its straightforward calculation and interpretation, there are many other ratios you can calculate to get a feel for whether a stock is cheap or expensive. Four of the most important are price to sales (P/S), price to book (P/B), dividend yield, and free-cash flow yield.

- Price to Sales (P/S). Just as it sounds, calculate this by dividing the price a company's shares sell for versus its revenue per share. There are two ways to calculate this ratio. Financial sites such as Yahoo! Finance will give you a company's market capitalization. "Market cap" for short, this is the price per share of the company multiplied by its total number of shares outstanding and is a measure of how much the total company is worth. You can divide the market capitalization by the annual revenue for the company, which you can find on the income statement. You can also calculate the sales per share first by dividing the total revenue by the number of shares outstanding, and then divide this by the stock price. P/S ratios can be useful for companies that currently have negative earnings. Care should be taken not to inappropriately compare ratios across industries, however, as the P/S ratio will depend on the nature of the business. A retailer like Wal-Mart that has extremely low profit margins will have a much smaller P/S ratio than a manufacturer like Apple.

- **Price to Book (P/B).** The "Book value" of a company is an accounting measure of the net investments it has made over its lifetime. The simplest way to think of it is as the total equity investment in the company to date, including initial capital from shareholders and reinvested profits in the course of the business' history.

This is the first ratio we have looked at that is based on a "balance sheet" measure of a company rather than an income statement measure. While the income statements represent the yearly "flows" of a company, the balance sheet is a measure of "stocks or the cumulative value of

60

those flows over time." When earnings flow in from the income statements, they initially increase a company's assets, which can be things like cash, property, land, and other investments. Similarly, when costs enter through the income statement, they appear as liabilities on a company's balance sheet. The difference between assets and liabilities is what we call "equity." Equity is an accounting measure of the value of shareholder investments. The "book" value in a P/B ratio is simply the value of equity.

This can be illustrated by an example. Imagine that a company raises $10,000 from investors and takes out another $10,000 in debt. It earns $5,000 in profits in its first year, which it reinvests into the business. At the end of the first year, the company will have $25,000 in assets ($10,000 + $10,000 + $5,000). From this $25,000 it spends $20,000 on a factory and has $5,000 in cash. You can think about book value in two ways. The first is the total amount of money that has been invested in the business by shareholders, which is the $10,000 initial investment plus the $5,000 of reinvested profits from the first year, or $15,000 total (the $10,000 in debt does not count since this is owed to bond holders or a bank). The second way is to think about what the balance sheet of the company would look like. Balance sheets provide useful measures of assets and liabilities. Assets are the things a company has that have real value or that can produce earnings in the future. Liabilities are the things that the company will have to pay for in the future. The balance sheet of our hypothetical company would look like this:

Assets   *Liabilities*

$5k cash   *$10k Debt*

$20k factory

For total assets of $25k and total liabilities of $10k, the difference in assets and liabilities, $15k, is the company's book value, which can be interpreted as the equity shareholders would have left over if the company ceased operations, sold off all of its assets, and paid back its liabilities.

The logic of the price/book ratio is easiest to see if you imagine that you are evaluating the purchase of a small business. One thing you would definitely want to know is what the business' assets are actually worth. If the net assets of the business are worth more than you would be paying for them (P/B < 1), you might be interested in buying the company just to get a hold of them. For instance, if you are considering buying a retail store, you might find that the value of the land, property, and inventory the store owns is greater than the price you would be paying for it. This can be the case for companies that own a lot of real estate at a time when land prices are going up significantly, as in the early part of this decade. In these cases, the land a company has on its books might be worth more than its stock price, so it would make sense for it simply to shut down its operations and sell off all of its assets. On the other hand, if a company was selling for many times the value of its net assets, you might wonder if it would be cheaper to start your own company from scratch.

P/B ratios are most often used when looking at companies in industries with lots of "real assets" and few "intangible" ones. Real assets are tangible things you can buy or sell, such as factories, equipment, and land. Intangible assets are things that have a lot of value but that you cannot buy or sell, such as brands, customer loyalty, and technology. Coca-Cola is a good example of a business with lots of intangible assets—a competitor could come along and build the same factories, but it would lack the incredibly valuable "Coke" brand name. Because of this, Coca-Cola (KO) has a very high price/book ratio (around 5).

- Dividend Yield ("Yield"). Going back to our original theory that the value of a stock is the current value of all expected future dividends, it might seem like it would make sense to look at a ratio of the stock price to current dividends. This is indeed something that analysts look at, though they usually flip it around and look at the dividend yield, which is the annual dividends per share divided by the stock price. This can be interpreted as the percentage of your initial investment that you will receive in income every year. For instance, if you are paying $20 for a stock and it has paid a $1 annual dividend for the past couple of years, you will get 5% of your money back every year. Again, you should compare this dividend yield to the market average, the industry average, and the average yield the company has had in the past.

A higher than average dividend yield could be a sign that a company looks cheap, but the reverse is not necessarily true. Many high-growth companies like Apple will decide not to pay dividends for a number of reasons. Sometimes they need to reinvest the money in their business in order to grow. Other times they just like to build up a cash reserve in case the economy goes south or they want to acquire another business. In other cases, the company might decide that buying back shares of its own stock is a more tax-

64

efficient way to give money back to its shareholders. This is because dividends are taxable distributions, so shareholders have to give a portion of them to the federal government. Buying back shares has some of the same effects as increasing dividends without the tax penalty, since it lowers the number of shares outstanding and therefore increases earnings and eventually dividends per share. It can also be a way to increase demand for the company's shares in the short term.

- **Free Cash Flow Yield (FCF).** Finally, just as valuing a company based on its free cash flows in a DCF analysis can be a good way to get around some of the difficulties of predicting a company's future dividend payout policy, so too can using an FCF yield be a good substitute for using a dividend yield. As a reminder, free cash flow is a company's cash flow from operations (CFO) minus capital expenditures. An FCF ratio is especially pertinent for large and mature companies such as GE or Wal-Mart. These companies should have relatively constant capital expenditures, so FCF may be a better measure of the actual cash that could be returned to shareholders than earnings or dividends. For younger and faster-growing companies that are still reinvesting much of their profits in future growth, the ratio might be less meaningful. These kinds of companies are still trying to grow their businesses and are not in "cash harvesting" mode just yet.

5.2. Other Critical Factors to Consider

This chapter will look at the factors that can effect what kind of ratio a company trades at, including a company's growth rate of earnings, its capital efficiency, and the quality of its balance sheet.

At the individual stock level, you should be careful not to assume that "cheap" automatically means "good stock to buy." There are many factors that can affect what kind of multiple a stock will command in the market. Three of the most important are the growth rate of earnings, the capital efficiency of the business (a measure of how much money they need to invest in order to get an additional $1 in earnings), and the balance sheet of the company. We will look at each of these in turn.

Growth Rate of Earnings

Imagine two companies that are each earning $10 a share today. Company A is selling at $300 for a PE multiple of 30, while company B is selling at $100 for a PE multiple of

10. Company A certainly looks "cheaper," but this does not necessarily mean that it is a better value to investors, just as a $99 TV is not automatically a better value than a $400 TV.

To see one hypothetical reason why, imagine that Company A is a young biotechnology firm that has recently filed a patent for a successful treatment of a common type of cancer, and imagine that Company B is a regulated utility company that provides gas and electric services to the regional Washington state area. Though these two companies might have similar earnings today, it is obvious that there is potential for company A to have much higher earnings in the future. Of course, the current shareholders of Company A will realize this and demand a higher price to sell their shares today because of it. Therefore, Company A will justifiably sell at a much higher PE multiple than Company B. Whether or not this represents "overpricing" or "value" depends on how successful you think Company A can be in the future. If Company B was in a dying industry (think horse and buggies when automobiles came along or typewriters at the advent of the personal computer) then it might justifiably trade at an even lower PE multiple.

So how can you tell how fast a company's earnings are going to grow in the future? It is very difficult, perhaps impossible, to make precise quantitative predictions with any accuracy. More important is having an understanding of the business and a view of whether fundamentals (sales) are going to improve or deteriorate in the future. This is one reason it can be helpful to go through the exercise of a DCF analysis even if you take the "final result" with a grain of salt. For a quick and dirty look at earnings growth, you can look at the trajectory of earnings over the past decade as well as Wall Street analysts' estimates of the company's earnings in the future. You can find estimates of this year's earnings as well as next year's earnings on popular sites like Yahoo! Finance. Of course, it is always essential to understand these estimates in the context of what is going on qualitatively in the business and the industry.

One "back of the envelope" way that analysts may try to incorporate a company's growth prospects into the PE multiple is looking at what is called a PEG (pronounced like the word "peg") ratio. This is simply the PE multiple divided by a company's expected 3-5 year earnings growth rate. So if Company A was supposed to grow earnings at a rate of 30% over the next 3-5 years, then it would have a PEG of 1. If Company B was only supposed to grow earnings at 5% over the same period, it would have a PEG of 2. Based on this ratio, Company A looks like the better buy, even though it has a much higher PE ratio. The PEG ratio is a very inexact measure, but it can be helpful in pointing out that companies that are growing at different rates should have different multiples.

Capital Efficiency

Though earnings are a very important metric, what you really want as a long-term shareholder is dividends, as we pointed out before. The ability of a company to convert earnings into dividends is partly dependent on how much of their earnings they need to reinvest each year in order to achieve their target rate of earnings growth. A company with very high capital efficiency will not need to make very many investments. A company with very low capital efficiency will have to invest a lot of money in plant, property, and machinery each year in order to sustain its business and produce more earnings.

Two good measures of capital efficiency are return on equity (ROE) and return on capital employed (ROCE). ROE can be found on most financial sites, or you can calculate it

70

by dividing the bottom-line net earnings of a company by its book (equity) value (the same value we used to calculate the price/book ratio in the previous chapter). ROCE can be calculated as *(Net Income + Interest Expense) / (Total Debt + Equity)*. Both of these ratios are measures of earnings (return) over total money invested. The logic is that companies that have produced high earnings per dollar invested will probably have to invest less in the future than companies that have produced relatively low earnings per dollar invested.

Two things are relevant about ROE: the absolute value and the trend. The absolute value should be above 10% for a "good" business. It is important that a company earns more on the money it invests than it has to pay (implicitly or explicitly) for access to that money. Since the denominator in ROE is equity, we should compare the ROE to the "cost" a company has to pay for its equity capital. Of course, there is no direct cost to the company from issuing more shares and taking in more money from shareholders, so the "direct cost of equity" is 0. However, since the stock market returns about 10% a year on average, we can think about there being a 10% "opportunity cost" to shareholders who have given up their money. This is because if earnings were given back to shareholders, they could reinvest the money in other stocks. Therefore, if you are purchasing a stock for more than the net assets of its books (in other words, the company has a P/B > 1), its ROE should be significantly greater than 10%. It follows that:

• A company that cannot earn an ROE of greater than 10% over the long term is effectively wasting its shareholders money. Its shareholders would be better off if it ceased operating, liquidated its assets, and returned the proceeds to the shareholders, who could reinvest it in companies with higher returns.

On the flipside, you should be willing to pay a slightly higher multiple for a company that has an ROE of above 20% than you would be for a company that is only at 10-15%. The higher-returning company will not have to invest as many earnings back into its business to produce growth, so shareholders will be able to "own" more of its profits.

In addition to the absolute value, the trend in ROE is very important because what you really care about as an investor is not what returns a company is earning today on investments that it has made in the past, but what returns a company will earn in the future on the incremental investments it is making today. A steadily improving ROE may be evidence that a company is earning high returns on the incremental capital invested even if the overall ROE looks poor because of unwise investments in the past. Similarly, a steadily falling ROE or ROCE may be evidence that a company is getting lower returns on its current investments than it was able to get in the past.

Balance Sheet

A final thing to note in interpreting any valuation ratio is the health of a company's balance sheet. Companies with very unhealthy balance sheets—think bank stocks in 2008—may trade at what appear to be very cheap valuations based on book value or earnings. What makes a balance sheet "unhealthy" can be subject to investor interpretation, but the general idea is that anytime the market questions a company's ability to continue to finance its businesses by raising capital, bad things will result.

Two things that can cause the market to begin to question a company's ability to finance its existing assets are large and growing debt and assets that are decreasing in value.

• **Large debt** is problematic because interest payments are usually a fixed cost, meaning that they do not vary based on revenue. So if earnings fall due to a recession or new competition entering the market, a company that has lots of debt may fail to generate the cash it needs to make its interest payments, resulting in bankruptcy. A company with less debt has more flexibility to survive a downturn since its fixed costs are lower.

• **Falling asset values** are problematic both because they will result in lower cash inflows in the future than anticipated and because in extreme cases they can cause lenders to question a company's solvency.

The first of these problems can be evaluated using more handy ratios. The second requires following news and press releases from a company and watching for anything that could require asset impairments. Some ratios to use to get a handle on how much debt a company has included:

• **Debt/Equity Ratio.** Calculate this from the balance sheet using (Short-term Debt + Long-term debt) / (Total Common Equity). The debt/equity ratio is a measure of how a company has historically financed its new operations. There are generally three choices: take out new debt, reinvest earnings, or issue new stock. The latter two are considered "equity" because they come directly or indirectly from shareholders. A debt/equity ratio of 1 or more indicates "significant" leverage. One above 3 is getting into a dangerous zone.

Debt/EBITDA. EBITDA is "Earnings before Interest, Taxes, Depreciation, and Amortization." Depreciation and amortization are added back because they are non-cash charges that reflect the deterioration in investments that a company has already made (such as the slow decay of a factory or piece of equipment). The logic of this ratio is that EBITDA is the maximum amount a company can put toward interest payments every year if it wants to completely cease expanding its business. A debt/EBITDA ratio of 4 or above is entering the "danger zone."

• **Interest Coverage, EBITDA/Interest Expense.** The most basic ratio, this measures the ability of a company to continue to make interest payments on its existing debt. It should be above 3 to be comfortable.

As an investor, you want to be acutely aware of staying on top of any balance sheet issues. Once the market decides that a company's balance sheet is in question, things can spiral downhill very fast due to a rather technical issue called "debt overhang." In simple terms, once a company's survival has been questioned, it can become very difficult for it to raise either debt or equity to make payments. This is because new investors will rationally fear that the new capital will just go to benefit existing investors by directly or indirectly paying back their claims.

6. Macro-Fundamental Strategies to Outperform the Market

Aspiring traders usually identify professional speculation with trend trading, price patterns, and the use of mechanical trading systems, but there are a number of successful stock traders that rely on fundamental analysis to guide their trade decisions.

Warren Buffett is probably the most famous fundamental trader in modern times, though he is not often considered as such. But if success comes from modeling the modern day masters of a given profession, Buffett is truly one of the masters in the trading universe.

Consider how he makes decisions about which companies he will invest in or buy outright. He analyzes whether a company has a true competitive advantage that acts as a protective "moat" from would-be competitors, and only then does he go through the painstaking process of analyzing a company's fundamentals and whether or not they meet his criteria. Once he has a firm understanding of how a company operates in its marketplace does he then put a number on the stock's price on where he would be a buyer of the stock.

Then he sits and waits patiently for the market to take a stock's price down to his buy point, at which time he buys aggressively.

Given his success, it stands to reason that fundamental trading is a reliable strategy to consider.

Let's explore some methods used by some very successful traders that you can consider for your own use.

Fundamental Strategy #1

Ray Dalio has one of the world's only systematic fundamental trading methods. In an interview in *Hedge Fund Market Wizards*, he says: Since the same fundamentals have different implications in different environments, markets will react differently in different environments to the same set of fundamentals. For example, the printing of money might not cause inflation during deleveraging, which goes against conventional belief. A systematic fundamental approach like this must be "timeless and universal" so that it analyzes the history of multiple markets around the world.

78

Dalio also mentions that changes in expected growth and inflation are the dominant drivers of asset classes. He offers a quadrant:

Growth increase Inflation increase	Growth increase Inflation decrease
Growth decrease Inflation increase	Growth decrease Inflation decrease

Lastly, Dalio states that correlation doesn't exist: one year the markets may be positively correlated, and the next year they may be negatively correlated. To quote *Hedge Fund Market Wizards*, "When economic growth expectations are volatile, stocks and bonds will be negatively correlated. When inflation expectations are volatile, stocks and bonds will be positively correlated." Correlation is simply the effect, not the cause. Investors say that they can't build a diversified portfolio because the markets are all correlated—not true. You can build a diversified portfolio by investing in markets that have different drivers.

This is a preliminary model of how Ray Dalio categorizes and analyzes market history:

Level 1: Categorize the country. Stage 1: Country is poor and thinks it's poor. Stage 2: Country is getting rich and thinks it's poor. Stage 3: Country is rich and thinks it's rich. Stage 4: Country is getting poor and thinks it's rich. Stage 5: Country is poor and thinks it's poor.

Level 2 (subcategory under Level 1): Categorize the country into a leveraging or deleveraging phase.

Level 3 (subcategory under Level 2): Categorize into Growth Increasing & Inflation Increasing, Growth Increasing & Inflation Decreasing, Growth Decreasing & Inflation Increasing, or Growth Decreasing & Inflation Decreasing.

The environments that Ray Dalio imposes above—growth, inflation, and leveraging/deleveraging—are all in the book *Hedge Fund Market Wizards*. Rather than analyzing history based on the environments Dalio provides us with, we should figure out *how* Dalio came up with these environments. Since Dalio has developed more environments than growth increase/decrease, inflation increase/decrease, and leverage/deleverage, we must find out *how* he determined which environments to use (because if you use the wrong categories, your model will be useless).

1. As a young trader, Dalio examined history: cycles, the economy, markets, political policies, etc.

2. He then grouped certain fundamentals together based on what kind of market price action they created (bull, bear, sideways).

3. He found that some fundamentals produced the same market price action. For example, inflation leads to increasing stock prices.

4. After more analysis, he found that, for example, Fundamental XYZ will in many cases produce a bull market, but in some cases it will not. That fundamental would produce a similar price action enough times to make you wonder about it, but it would also baffle you because there were some situations in which it produced an unexpected price action.

5. He categorized the fundamentals in even more detail. For example, he split Fundamental XYZ, producing a bull

market in a different category than that of Fundamental XYZ, producing a bear market.

6. After examining the two groups mentioned above in more detail, he determined the reason why Fundamental XYZ would in some cases produce a bull market and in some cases a bear market (e.g., growth, inflation, leverage/deleverage).

7. After repeating the above steps, he found that the reason that other fundamentals such as Fundamental ABC could produce different price actions was *also* because of things like growth, inflation, and leverage/deleverage.

8. Thus, after seeing the same characteristics (growth, inflation, leverage/deleverage) show up over and over again, he concluded that these were the environments on which he could analyze historical markets.

9. After he created a model based on economic environments, he was able to use deductive reasoning (use a general conclusion to obtain a conclusion regarding a specific event), whereas before he was using inductive reasoning.

For example, Ray Dalio found that inflation would cause stocks to go up. But he also found that inflation has caused prices to fall in the past. Why? After further categorization, he found that the reason inflation sometimes causes prices to rise and sometimes causes prices to fall is because of, for example, leverage/deleveraging—this leverage is the dividing line that causes the same fundamental to have different market implications.

The problem with this style

Ray Dalio employs 1,400 people to analyze the fundamentals of multiple markets throughout history so that his model is "timeless and universal." Because historical events have similar characteristics, he is able to predict the future with stunning accuracy.

Problem:

1. This strategy requires a massive amount of human resources, which is why Dalio hires so many people. Only after analyzing a ton of markets throughout history will such a model be of any predictive use. One person cannot do the work of 1,400.

2. It's very hard to identify what the *real* fundamental factors are.

3. With so many factors at play, it is very difficult to predict which fundamental factor will override the other fundamentals when the trend isn't clear.

5. The biggest problem: many times, you don't know what the fundamentals are—you only see the price action. In other words, we only see the effect (bull/bear market), not the cause (the fundamentals).

Let me give you an example. How could anyone have known that the reason for the 1970s silver bull market was a cornering operation by the Hunt brothers? No one could have known. How would anyone have known that the Harry brothers were secretly cornering gold? Only after the bull market was over was it evident that the Hunt brothers had tried to corner silver.

Solution:

We'd love to trade the way Ray Dalio does, but at the moment, trading *solely* based on the fundamentals like Dalio won't work for us. When you have the money to hire employees, you'll be able to do what he does. But that doesn't mean we shouldn't pay attention to the fundamentals. A good trader always has the macro picture in the back of his mind. As Angela Zhou says, "Trade like a technical, think like a fundamental."

George Soros loves to say "trade first, investigate later." By this, he's saying that when you don't understand the fundamental reason for the price move, just use the technicals to trade it.

Note: Jim Roger's trading style is similar to Dalio's. Rogers analyzes historical cycles and finds commonalities. Rogers was able to do this when he first started trading because the world was a lot smaller and easier to understand in the 1970s. There were fewer complicating factors, such as China, to consider.

Fundamental Strategy #2

Colm O'Shea's fundamental strategy is simple: instead of predicting the future fundamentals, just recognize them when they appear. How does simply recognizing reality give you an edge? The market often ignores reality.

1. Recognize a divergence between the real fundamental situation and what the market wants to see.

2. Don't put on a trade yet. Investors can carry on their disbelief for a long time, and as long as no one cares, the market will not converge with the fundamentals.

3. Keep trading on the side of the market hysteria until it ends, even when you can clearly see that the fundamentals and the market have diverged.

4. Wait until people are forced to notice the fundamentals. That this is a good idea is evidenced by volatility spikes. Wait until people start to care. Then put on the trade.

5. The key isn't knowing that a trade is correct, but *knowing that the trade is correct right now.*

His strategy only works for major market turning points, when the fundamentals and price diverge. This is a discretionary (non-systematic) fundamental trading style.

Here is a key component of this strategy: "What is important to the market isn't whether growth is good or bad,

86

but whether it is getting better or worse. 2009, Growth started getting less negative, and less negative is good news. 2009: the economy stopped getting worse, and the markets started going up. The underlying problems hadn't gone away, but that isn't the market driver."

Here's an example. The Euro problem has never been solved. At seemingly random times, the Euro will tank and European interest rates will skyrocket, not because the Euro problem has suddenly gotten massively worse—the problem's been there all along—but because all of a sudden the people start to notice. As long as people don't care, there is no problem. However, the day will come when people are forced to care because reality has strayed too far from belief.

A key component of this strategy is that the market doesn't care whether growth is good or bad—it cares whether growth is getting better or worse. In mid-2009, some people shorted the market because "the economy was still bad." Thus, using Colm O'Shea's strategy, they saw a divergence between the fundamentals and the market. However, what they didn't realize is that growth getting less negative and the economy not getting worse are solid reasons for the market to go up. The economy was still bad, but it was getting better.

Recognizing Fundamentals

As Colm O'Shea states, you only have to recognize the fundamentals when they appear. But how can you recognize the current fundamentals as soon as possible?

The problem with most economic indicators (besides a few, such as railroad indicators) is that they lag behind the real situation. Many indicators are released a month or more after the period is over (e.g., November's data is released in late December). Pretty useless by the time you get it, isn't it? Here's the solution to this problem:

1. Pay attention to a couple of people who like to speak out, are connected to the business community, and have good track records, such as Jack Welch.

2. Pay attention to serious thinkers who have good track records, such as Ray Dalio, Jeremy Grantham, Jeff Gundlach, and Jim Rogers.

3. Pay special attention when someone who speaks out says something that goes against the trend. For example, by February 2009 all the big banks said that "things were

actually not as bad as expected." Pay attention, because they weren't lying. They put their reputations on the line by putting this out in the open.

4. For people like Warren Buffett who are often bullish ("Don't Bet Against America," etc.), you can discount what he says when he's bullish. But if he's bearish (an anomaly), you should pay attention to what he's saying.

Mixed Fundamentals

In the middle part of a secular bear market, the fundamentals are mixed. People say that the middle section of a bear market is extremely irrational; on the contrary, it's very rational if you look at it this way.

The market needs a theme to dominate its mindset, regardless of how trivial this theme/topic really is. This theme can be negative or positive. It doesn't matter because in a secular bear market, it's easy to find a billion negative and a billion positive factors. Think of it as a relay race: the same runners (negative/positive) need to pass on the baton to a new runner. For example, the market will focus on a negative theme for a while, but soon the market will need to find a *new* negative theme because it can only play the same theme for so long. If it can't find a negative theme, it will try to find a positive theme. Once a positive theme is found, the market will play that theme for a while and then search for a new positive theme. And the cycle goes on.

This cycle is reinforced by media networks like CNBC. For example, the market moves, and then the media networks scramble to find a fundamental reason (theme) to explain it (because if they can't find a reason, they'll look like incompetent idiots). There's a host of themes to choose from, and the media networks can pick any one of them, regardless of how trivial they are. The masses read the headlines and jump on the bandwagon, reinforcing the cycle.

A good example is the recent "news" about Spanish corruption. The media attributed this (the "re-emergence of the Euro problem") to the recent rise in Spanish interest rates. The news doesn't make the market—the market makes the news. Spanish rates started rising in mid-January 2013, half a month before this corruption was revealed.

About Expectations

What's important isn't what the real macro situation is—it's what investors focus on. Thus, in every market, there are two areas: the real fundamental situation and what the market is expecting (this is evident from market price).

When investors' expectations are way out of touch with reality, the market will tank if reality underperforms expectations by even just a little bit (and vice versa). It is very easy for reality to come in as slightly different from expectations, because expectations are extremely positive (or negative), which leaves a lot of room on the other end of the spectrum for reality to come in.

Let me give you an example. Say investors are way too optimistic about the housing recovery (expectations). They expect a V-shaped recovery, which isn't possible because it goes against the nature of the housing market (bottoms are long and drawn out). This optimism is evident in homebuilders' stocks, which are close to their 2007 highs. In addition, sentiment is way too high, as housing confidence is near its 2007 peak. When the upcoming housing data is released, the market will tank if the data even slightly underperforms their expectations. And this slight underperformance is very likely to occur because expectations have become extremely unrealistic.

Even the world's foremost housing expert, Robert Shiller, mentions this:

"I don't think a boom is in the cards. We might see home prices go up a little bit, you know, a little bit above inflation, maybe. Not likely that we'll see a real boom. You know, I don't quite see it. It's not this gung-ho, going into housing."

Economists' theories as to why Fundamental XYZ should produce a bull/bear market are useless because they can give you a million economic calculations describing how the markets will go up just as easily as they can give you calculations describing how the markets will go down. At the end of the day, it's cycles (time) that determine where the market will go.

Here's an example. By economic theory, QE4 (fourth round of quantitative easing announced on September 13, 2012) should have made stocks skyrocket, because QE4 is "unlimited QE." Well, guess what? The announcement of QE4 happened exactly one day before the market top. Talk about selling on the news.

Now these economists are all scratching their chins and asking "What the hell happened?" By theory, QE4 injects "unlimited amounts of money into the economy, thereby causing prices to skyrocket, etc." But like I said, cycles (and by extension, nature's laws) conquer all. Nature's law is that if you keep injecting the same medicine over and over, its effectiveness wears off. Every consecutive round of QE has caused weaker and shorter (time-wise) market growth than the previous round.

Another example is the surge of Japanese Yen in late 2012. The new Japanese prime minister avidly supported aggressive monetary easing. By economic theory, this new monetary easing should be useless, because Japan has been doing the same thing for the past twenty years without any effect! So why is the Yen all of a sudden depreciating so quickly? Cycles. Japan's bear market has lasted twenty years already. All cycles end in 17-20 years time.

7. How to Interpret Price Action

"Do not use the words 'Bullish' or 'Bearish.' These words fix a firm market-direction in the mind for an extended period of time. Instead, use 'Upward Trend' and 'Downward Trend' when asked the direction you think the market is headed. Simply say: 'The line of least resistance is either upward or downward at this time.' Remember, don't fight the tape!" - Jesse Livermore

Today, some of the most successful traders adapt some kind of set of rules for identifying price trends to their trading because trend trading is one of the most reliable trading methods ever developed.

But even if most aspiring traders realize that, and if trend trading is so reliable, why do so many fail at making money with it?

Most of the time, it's an inability to read price action properly, which causes many traders to lack the ability to identify price trends.

I'm going to outline in great detail how to identify price trends effectively, but there is something essential to your trading success that I need to share with you first.

Critical components of successful speculation are your trade criteria and your trading method. Trade criteria is what type of underlying security you are going to trade and the conditions that must be met before you actually trade.

Before you pull the trigger on a trade and take an entry, you have to know what you'll be trading as well as how to read the conditions that must be present before you take a position so that you can put the odds in your favor.

When your criteria are present, your trading method will actually guide you in identifying the trade setup, pulling the trigger, and managing the trade.

But you can't blame your average trader for missing the clues. We typically think of markets as "up" or "down" entities, with little consideration for timeframe or directional movement across periods. This brings us to an important concept in recognizing the operative state of the market. If you change your point of reference, price trends take on a whole new shape.

Time Periods

Time periods are generally defined as follows:

- Long-term: A period of months to years.
- Intermediate-term: A period of weeks to months.
- Short-term: A period of minutes to days or weeks.

A critical rule when using time periods is that the larger timeframe has dominance over the smaller time period when defining primary price movement.

By understanding time periods, you can define the period of price action to determine which market type is in play. The markets types are simply up, down, and sideways. Once you can properly identify the market type, you can tailor your approach for higher performance.

Warren Buffett's style of value investing—described as "selective contrarian investing" in *The New Buffettology*—focuses not just on buying stock on valuation but instead on actively exploiting bear markets as primary buying opportunities. For Buffett, the shift to a down market is a key setup for bargains to ultimately materialize. This market type is an important condition for maximizing returns.

Courtesy of FreeStockCharts.com

Figure 1 - Short-term timeframe.

To analyze price action, you need to be able to classify it into one of three time periods: short-term, intermediate-term, or long-term. Short-term trends last from a few minutes to a few days, intermediate-term trends last from a week to several months, and long-term trends last from several months to years.

In addition, trends will begin to form depending on whether the underlying security is under active accumulation or distribution. Accumulation occurs when a stock or commodity is being acquired by a sufficient number of investors and the market reflects a gradual increase in price because of rising demand. This is indicated by a steady series of higher-highs and higher-lows.

Conversely, distribution occurs when a stock or commodity is being sold as a sufficient number of investors liquidate their holdings. This results in a gradual price decline as demand for it falls, leading to a steady succession of lower-highs and lower-lows.

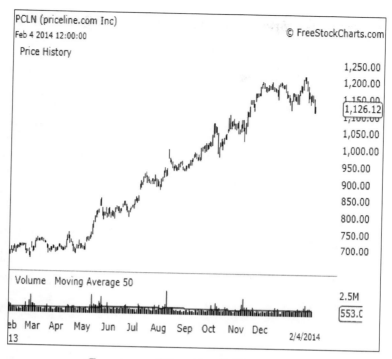

Courtesy of FreeStockCharts.com

Figure 2 – Intermediate-term timeframe.

If price is not exhibiting either of these behaviors—upward
or downward movement—then it is consolidating in a
trading range until an imbalance is created in either supply
or demand, and it will remain in consolidation until either
the bulls or the bears gain control and force a trend to
emerge. The game changer is when an external force, or
catalyst, enters the market and changes the dynamic of the

direction of the trend, which will be revealed in the trend's price action.

If more traders understood this concept and knew how to react to it, they might have avoided the crash and instead have adopted or developed tools that would have made money as prices churned.

Courtesy of FreeStockCharts.com
Figure 3 – Long-term timeframe.

100

7.1. Fundamentals of Price Trends

"The trend is your friend except at the end when it bends."

- Ed Seykota, master trader, trend follower, profiled in *Market Wizards*

To understand price action at its most basic level, you can condense it down into two fundamental types: contraction and expansion.

Like the Yin Yang symbol in Chinese culture, these two forces are always at work, and while it may appear that one is fighting for dominance over the other, the seed of each side is contained in the other. The markets can't work or achieve any type of harmony or balance without both aspects of contraction and expansion at work.

When markets are contracting, it's fairly obvious from the price action on a chart because price is neutral, or range bound, and will typically fluctuate between two price points or within a certain range.

Trading ranges or developing chart patterns are signs that price contraction is taking place.

Price trends are indicative of expansion where price movement is clearly moving in a given direction.

Go and pull up a stock chart and then input any stock symbol, hit enter, and what appears next will seem to be a long series of erratic lines that mean nothing to most people but everything to an experienced trader. The lines are the stock's price action and tell you where the stock has traded in the past as well as where it is currently trading.

Courtesy of FreeStockCharts.com

Figure 1

The lines can be in the form of candlesticks, price bars, or a composite line that is the sum of the stock's opening, closing, and daily price range, but no matter which form price action takes on the chart in front of you, it is a form of communication between the stock and yourself.

Price action is a type of language that speaks to those who make an effort to hear it. If you take time to master the basics in the form of price, volume, and using a set of simple technical tools, then you have the means to translate price action into actionable events that you can exploit for profit.

Think of it this way: if you were in a burning building and the only other person there was a foreigner from another country who didn't speak a word of English and you had just minutes to try to communicate on how to work together in order to get out and reach safety, how would you talk to that person?

You could motion him to follow, try to read his body language, pick up on the tonality of his voice when says certain words to derive their emotional meaning, you could try universal sign language, etc.

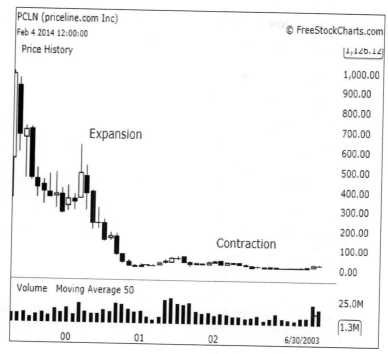

Courtesy of FreeStockCharts.com

Figure 2

With price action, you look at where the stock's price has traveled, which direction it is pointed toward, turning points, technical indicators to help translate overbought/oversold conditions, and complimentary technical indicators to help keep you in sync with price action's next step.

The reason you should learn how to read price action is fundamental to trading—to find trends.

Trading trends are to trading what air is to you and me—it is the stuff of life for a trader, namely profits.

There is no simpler way to stay on the path to profitability than being able to identify trends in price movement and then simply stepping in front of it and riding that trend profitably.

Now, this is simpler said that done for most people, because while everyone knows that "the trend is your friend," the sad fact is that most people go about it all wrong, which is why the success rate for profitable trading is so low. Those who do succeed often suffer through an incredibly long learning curve, but, fortunately, the goal of this book is to help you avoid that.

So, first, what is a trend? A trend is when the price action of an underlying security is moving steadily in a given direction based on its time period.

For a bullish trend, when price action is trading upward, price action should be making a steady series of higher-highs and higher-lows as it trades higher.

For a bearish trend, price action is trading downward and making a steady series of lower-highs and lower-lows in its price action.

When price stops moving in a given direction, it is neutral, or range bound, meaning there is no real direction in its price movement.

This is a basic explanation that will be expanded on in this book for you a little later, but for now, just understand that you want to become a student of price action because it will help you define the trend in an underlying security's (stock, currency, commodity, etc.) price action, which will help you become more profitable by trading in the direction of its price movement.

The reason trading with the trend will lead to long-term, out-sized returns for you is that trend trading closely parallels Isaac Newton's First Law of Motion:

An object at rest stays at rest and an object in motion stays in motion with the same speed and in the same direction unless acted on by an unbalanced force.

When price is in motion—bullish or bearish—Newton's First Law applies because a price trend tends to stay in motion, only pausing to pull back before resuming its direction. In trading, the reason this often occurs is that when price pulls back, it's because traders are taking profits, but then other traders will pile on and start buying.

There are lots of reasons why this happens, but the most common reason is that sellers often get in early on the trend while other traders are either late to the game or overly cautious and wait for the trend to prove itself before risking any capital. When price pulls back, early traders sell and take profits while the other traders take positions in order to not miss out on the opportunity to get in.

Almost a self-fulfilling prophecy, the trend begins to resume its original path again.

This occurs over and over until a stronger force comes along and forces a game changer on the status quo, forcing a trend reversal.

By studying price action and using a few simple tools and methods, you'll know when this situation is likely to occur and how to adjust your position to protect your gains.

So keep reading.

7.2. How to Label Market Turns for Trend Trading

Because trends are the greatest source for profitable trades, your goal as a trader is to use all of your resources to hone in on and identify them.

Earlier, you read about how trends are identified—bullish, bearish, and neutral— depending on their movement at any given time. In this section, you're going to learn how to label turns in the market—price highs and price lows—in order to know what trend is in place, when the trend is in effect, or when it is changing.

Knowing how to label turns gives you the ability to navigate your way through the market and make adjustments based on what price action is telling you at any given moment.

As a reminder, when price action is trading upward, price action should be making a steady series of higher-highs and higher-lows as it trades higher.

110

A bearish trend is trading downward and making a steady series of lower-highs and lower-lows in its price action.

When price stops moving in a given direction, it is neutral, or range bound, where there is no real direction in its price movement.

Like a set of stairs that are stacked on top of one another to help people reach an upper floor (bullish) or a lower floor (bearish), price trends build up in a similar fashion. While not as symmetrical as a staircase, price movement can be labeled at each "step" in order help you gain a sense of the trend in place so that you can trade with greater confidence while also having the ability to know when a trend's movement is in question.

So, with a bullish trend, when price trades higher than the previous price high and then pulls back from that high, you want to label that price point an "HH," for higher-high. When price pulls back and then resumes its upward price movement, you want to take note of the price low; if that price low is higher than the previous price low prior to this one, you want to label it an "HL," for higher-low.

As long as price continues to make a steady series of higher-highs and higher-lows in its price action, it helps to know when the bulls are in control of the trend and to adjust your trades accordingly.

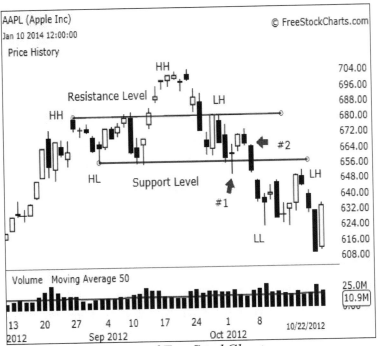

Courtesy of FreeStockCharts.com

Fig. 1

Here you can see Apple making a steady series of higher-highs and higher-lows until price begins to decline. At Point #1, the bullish bias was still in effect, despite trading below the previous low. Not until Point #2 when price closed below the previous price low did an actual confirmation take place, indicating that the bears were now in control.

112

For bearish trends, when price trades lower than the previous price low and then pulls back from that low, you want to label that price point an "LL" for lower-low in the price trend. When price pulls back and then resumes its downward price movement, you want to take notice of the price high, and if it's lower than the previous price high, you label it as an "LH" for lower-high in the price trend.

Bearish price trends are in force when they make a steady series of lower-lows and lower-highs in their price action and let you know that bears are in control of the trend, meaning it's best to trade to the short side in the direction of the downward trend.

What if the signals are mixed? What if you have a higher-high followed by a lower-low? What if you have a lower-low followed by a higher-high? Does it change the trend? Do you exit the trade?

Price is dynamic and always in a state of flux, so it's easy to get mixed signals and be left in a state of confusion. However, there are some guidelines to help you along the way.

If there is a bullish trend in effect, for example, and that trend is making a steady series of higher-highs and higher-lows but then price falters and forms a lower-high in price, the bullish trend is still technically in effect until the downward price action closes below the previous price low. If it touches it but fails to close below it, then the bullish trend is still in effect.

Even if it does close below the previous price low, this doesn't necessarily mean that the current trend is in full reversal but only that you need to adjust your strategy to account for any possible change. This is where good trade management comes into play as you sell part or all of your position as well as adjust your stop loss to adjust for the changing price dynamics.

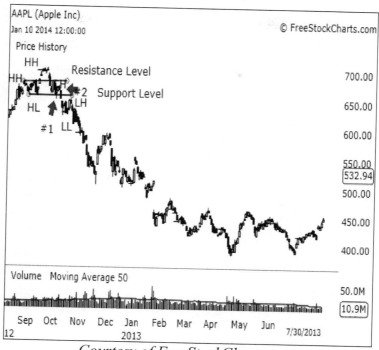

Courtesy of FreeStockCharts.com
Fig. 2

After the price reversal was confirmed at Point #2, a steady series of lower-highs and lower-lows followed, showing that the bears were firmly in charge.

The same is true for bearish trends.

For neutral or range bound markets, it's a bit different. You label the price turns, but since price is going back and forth, you have to identify support and resistance to trade price between those two points if that's your goal.

To summarize, a change in trend doesn't occur until price closes above or below the previous turning point in a security's price action.

At the same time, you have to look for signs of a breakout from that range by factoring in the relationship between price and volume.

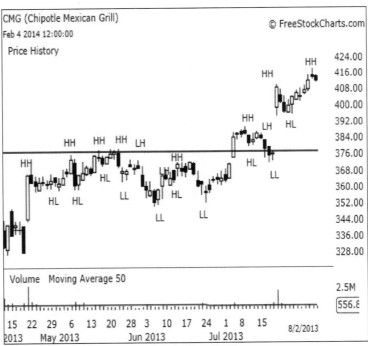

Courtesy of FreeStockCharts.com

Fig. 3

As CMG entered a period of price contraction in the form of a trading range, there were several market turns that offered a mixed bag of results. When price enters these types of contraction phases, you have to step back and look at the bigger picture in order not to get confused. If you find yourself confused, step aside and don't trade. Wait until price makes its direction apparent before risking any capital.

7.3. Price & Volume

While trading trends has been one of the most reliable methods devised for profitable trading, at some point all good things must end, including trends.

Price reversals can be brutal and sudden, because when an existing mature trend is in place, it can catch complacent traders off guard, as if they were hit by a sucker punch.

The reason is that no matter how strong a trend is or how long it has been in place, it cannot outrun its underlying fundamentals. Like a rubber band that has been stretched to its limit, at some point it will snap back quickly in the opposite direction.

In a fast-moving market, not knowing when a price reversal will appear is like playing Russian roulette. Even if you get lucky five times, when the hammer falls, you are finished.

Traders quickly turn into casualties due to an inability to read warning signs and make adjustments because they don't understand the relationship between price and volume. This can cause unnecessary losses as well as cause missing opportunities if a new trend emerges.

Trade volume is the total number of buy and sell transactions on a given underlying security during a given time period. Trade volume is to a stock's price movement what rocket fuel is to the space shuttle: it is the fuel of its price movement.

Daily trade volume counts, where you take notice of the number of transactions traded on a daily basis, are the most common measurement of a security.

Price and volume are like two sides of the same coin.

When a stock is trading higher, you will notice that volume spikes at key points in the stock's climb and usually at new price highs. When the average volume is increasing over time, the stock is considered to be under accumulation. Accumulation is when investors—both large and small— are buying up shares at a steady clip and the law of supply and demand kicks in where the limited amount of shares are increasing in value due to demand.

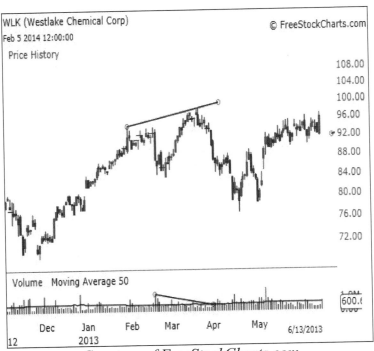

Fig. 1

WLK was trending higher but volume was declining at key price levels. When price and volume are moving away from each other, a reversal might be in the making, and it's a sign to get out or trade the other way.

When a stock is trading lower, you'll also notice large spikes in volume as the stock makes new price lows. When price is declining and the average trade volume is increasing, the stock is under distribution. Distribution is when a stock is being sold off and the law of supply and demand kicks in where a given amount of shares in are low demand and must be sold at bargain prices to make them attractive to a limited supply of buyers.

As you can see, price and volume tend to move in tandem with one another. When the two begin to diverge away from one another is when the stage is set for a potential reversal of the trend.

For example, when a stock is flying high, there is a risk that there won't be any more buyers at a particular price level. When that happens, volume tends to dry up, and then the investors who bought at those levels have no one else to sell to and there are no more investors to buy from. Trade volume dries up and price begins to falter because investors are getting scared.

Courtesy of FreeStockCharts.com
Fig. 2

ARWR was experiencing a long period of price contraction, but the stock's average volume began to rise. At the upper end of its trading range, ARWR broke out on 7-17-13 in a surge of volume almost 700% of its 50-day average. Stagnant stocks about to explode higher will often see their volume levels slowly begin to rise as large investors begin to accumulate shares, which indicates that a big move is underway.

Once the bulls figure out that they are the last investors to hold the bag, the scared money begins to sell, which begets more selling, and then a flood of selling sets in. Volume spikes up to record levels and price begins to roll over to the downside.

It works the same way with a bear market.

Eventually, everyone sells off their holdings, which culminates in a last heave of selling at the bottom as the last of the investors sell off all their holdings. It is at these levels that investors swear off the stock market, but smart traders recognize the spike in volume at the bottom as a signal to step in.

It is at these extreme levels that panic can set in, and by observing trade volume you can determine when the tide is shifting and when to get out or reverse your position.

Price convulses downward in a seeming death spiral just as the smart money steps in and buys at bargain prices. With all the sellers out of the market, the bulls seize control, and price and volume move in lockstep with one another as an upward trend finds support and begins moving north once again.

Fig. 3

PCLN suffered a big price decline followed by a huge price gap on 8-8-12 on volume that was at 140% of its fifty-day average, reaching a price low of around $556 a share. Afterward, price tried to climb higher but soon rolled over to test support at the $556 level. Support held as volume dried up, showing that the bears had exhausted themselves as price and volume diverged away from each other, allowing them to take control of the trend once again.

.

The study of price and volume is a cornerstone of technical analysis and successful trading. Using this data in

124

conjunction with the other tools listed in this book can give you a key competitive advantage over other traders and the tools to profit. More importantly, it can give you the tools to avoid getting caught flat-footed when the market goes against you.

7.4. Price Patterns

A price pattern occurs in a chart when price data is graphed where it naturally occurs and repeats over a given time period.

Visual patterns form due to the behavior of the individuals that make up the majority of the buying and selling of a particular underlying security. These patterns can be visually identified and capitalized on by a skilled trader.

Price patterns can be used as either reversal or continuation signals and are one of the basic tenets of technical analysis, though there are skeptics. Many economists have pointed out that the use of price patterns is little more than "reading tea leaves" and that there is no way to predict what the stock market will do based on price patterns alone.

I agree in part that price patterns alone cannot predict the market, but then again, economists have no foolproof way to predict the market either. I am confident that you can interpret price movement based on price patterns, not only because of my own experience but because of the experiences of many of the world's most successful traders (many of whom are profiled in Jack Schwager's *Market Wizard* series based on his interviews with the world's greatest traders).

I would also like to point out that William O'Neil, founder of *Investor's Business Daily* and author of *How to Make Money in Stocks*, has determined that the highest performing stocks in history formed key price patterns prior to massive run-ups in price.

A couple of things: First, there is an endless variety of information on the subject of price patterns. You'll see texts on how to spot everything from a dead cat bounce to an Iron Butterfly and delve into the esoteric study of planetary alignment.

Do yourself a favor and remember to keep it simple.

A lot of authors are selling these types of studies, and I even own quite a few of them. While they make for interesting reading, the fact is that if you complicate your trading, you're likely to fail.

Real price pattern trading is pragmatic and works in conjunction with the overall market's price movement and underlying fundamentals. If you combine these key factors with sound technical analysis, you'll be more profitable at the end of the day.

Next, we will go over in detail some of the key price patterns that will help you profit from your trading.

Cup & Handle Pattern

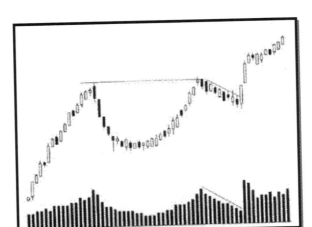

A Cup & Handle pattern is one of the most common consolidation patterns that forms during a contraction in price action (it is also my favorite pattern to trade, as the moves often explode in price for huge gains), which usually occurs after an extended move in price. Price action will move slowly down and then up in a U-shaped "cup."

Once the prior resistance level on the left side of the cup is met on the right side, prices will drift lower on decreasing volume until the upside breakout is triggered.

Cup & Handle patterns typically take 7 weeks to form, but some can take much longer (as long as a year), so be sure to look at the weekly and monthly charts to spot them and avoid missing any opportunities.

The handle, however, will take at least a week to form.

Identify the top resistance line of the cup and the subsequent resistance line of the handle. The price target will be approximately the depth of the cup to the upside past the cup resistance level by more than 10-15% before attempting a breakout.

The success rate of this pattern is 74% without volume confirmation, but with heavy volume of around 150% of normal volume with price breaking out to the upside, the success rate rises to 90%.

Flat Base Pattern

Bullish Flat Base Pattern

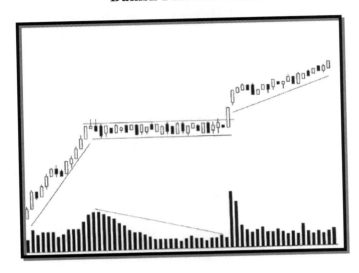

A Bullish Flat Base pattern is a continuation pattern usually occurring after an extended upward move in price. Price action will move in a very flat, sideways pattern after establishing a resistance level; this pattern is also referred to as a "high, tight flag." The unique characteristic of this pattern is the extended, nearly horizontal price action with decreasing volume before the breakout.

Now, this pattern can take up to three months to consolidate. Volume will typically dry up after hitting the resistance level, and the price will consolidate horizontally.

Greater than 150% of normal price volume is normally required to break out of the pattern to the upside.

Additionally, as with any horizontal base pattern, false breakouts accompanied by weak volume are common. I have a couple of tips that can help minimize your chances of getting whipsawed in a false breakout that will be covered a little later. These are based on a study on the highest-performing stocks (both bullish and bearish) in the last 100 years that revealed that there were key signals that will help you pick only the highest-probability entries on the best-moving stocks.

So, identify the support and resistance lines of the pattern. False breakouts to the upside are common at the resistance line, creating "bull traps" for those traders not patient enough to wait for the required volume confirmation to break out of the pattern. Breakouts should cause an explosive price movement out of the pattern, on average a 63% gain in price from the resistance level!

The success rate for this pattern alone is a respectable 68%, rising to a very respectable 83% if you wait for the confirmation on the breakout above the resistance level.

This is one of my favorite patterns, as well as hedge fund manager, radio personality, and author of "The Investor's Edge", Gary Kaultbaum's (who trades contracted base patterns similar to this one almost exclusively in his $200-million-plus hedge fund), and while the percentages are based on Thomas Bulkowski's work, I find that the percentages are much higher when you match this method's approach to stock selection and profiling combined with sticking to the strongest stocks in the strongest sector as well as moving in tandem with the general market. I've seen and experienced many stocks doubling or tripling in price coming out of these patterns, especially combining these steps with the entry methods you're going to read about a little later on.

Flag Patterns

Bull Flag Pattern

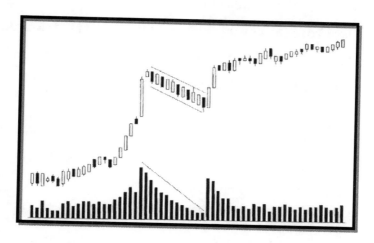

A Bull Flag pattern is another continuation pattern that occurs during a period of price contraction, usually after a large run-up in price (the run-up is often identified as the "flagpole" of this pattern). After a brief consolidation in the "flag" with decreasing volume, the trend will usually continue in the same direction as the previous trend.

The price target for the next run-up in price is approximately the same vertical distance as the previous flagpole.

Solid bull flag patterns generally break out to the upside

within 12 days. Formation longer than this generally resolves into Symmetrical Triangles or Wedges.

False breakouts are common with this pattern; price will rise above the upper trendline of the flag and return back down into the flag pattern within the day if more than 150% of normal volume does not accompany the breakout.

Keep track of the upper trendline of the flag pattern. Traders should enter long when this upper trendline is pierced on a valid breakout on heavy volume.

The success rate for this pattern is 87% if the breakout is confirmed with 150% greater than normal volume.

Bear Flag Pattern

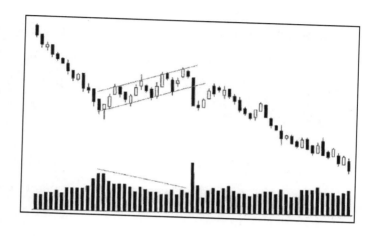

A Bear Flag pattern is another continuation pattern that occurs during a period of price contraction, usually after a large downward move in price (the large downward move is often identified as the "flagpole" of this pattern). After a brief consolidation in the "flag" with decreasing volume, the trend will usually continue in the same direction as the previous trend.

The price target for the next downward move in price is approximately the same vertical distance as the previous flagpole.

Solid Bull Flag patterns generally breakout to the upside within 3 weeks.

False breakouts are common with this pattern; price will fall below the lower trendline of the Flag and return back down into the Flag pattern within the day if more than 150% of normal volume does not accompany the breakout.

Keep track of the lower trendline of the Flag pattern. Traders should enter short when this lower trend line is pierced on a valid breakdown on heavy volume of 150% of normal volume or greater.

The success rate for this pattern is 88% if the breakdown is confirmed.

Triangles

Bullish Ascending Triangle Pattern

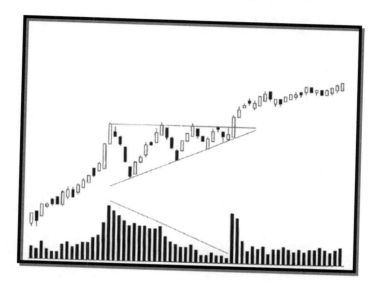

This triangle pattern is formed during periods of contraction in a stock's price action and usually occurs when there is a pause in a stock's price action after a breakout or a huge run-up. These patterns are formed either during a correction or during a consolidation of a stock's price and typically have a drop-off in trading volume while forming.

Price targets can be calculated by measuring the vertical

distance of the open end of the triangle. If you are following an explosive stock, you can always use a trailing stop loss to capture more of the move, depending on your preference.

The drop-in volume for this pattern is followed by a huge spike in volume that reveals that buyers are rushing onto the market for this stock. This spike in volume confirms the trade as price breaks through the upper trend line of the triangle. The success rate for this trade rises to 98% with a confirmation of volume.

Bearish Descending Triangle Pattern

A Descending Triangle pattern is another continuation pattern and is the counterpart of the Ascending Bullish Triangle pattern. It occurs during a pause in price action after a large decline in price. This pattern is formed either during a correction or a consolidation of a stock's price and typically has a drop-off in trading volume while forming.

Price targets can be calculated by measuring the vertical distance of the open end of the triangle. If you are following an explosive stock, you can always use a trailing stop loss to capture more of the move, depending on your preference.

The drop in volume for this pattern is followed by a huge

spike in volume that reveals that sellers are rushing onto the market to short sell the stock. This spike in volume confirms the trade as price breaks down through the lower trendline of the triangle. The success rate for this trade rises to 96% with a confirmation of volume.

It is common in a pattern like this for price to come back and retest the upper portion of the lower trendline after a price breakdown, which should act as resistance before the stock's price resumes its downward move. Some traders get nervous about this, but there is no need for it. This retest can actually be used to your advantage as a pullback trade in the event that you miss the initial breakdown move in price.

Bullish Symmetrical Triangle Pattern

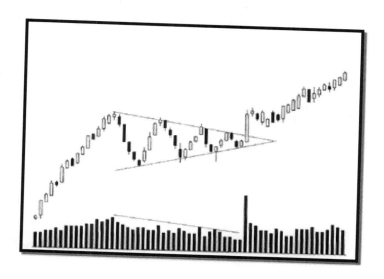

This continuation pattern typically occurs after a large increase in price. After price goes through consolidation or correction, this chart pattern begins to form with a decrease in volume, while the trend will usually continue in the same direction just before it begins to contract.

Price targets can be calculated by measuring the vertical distance of the open end of the triangle. If you are following an explosive stock, you can always use a trailing stop loss to capture more of the move, depending on your preference.

The drop in volume for this pattern is followed by a huge spike in volume that reveals that buyers are rushing onto the market for this stock. This spike in volume confirms the trade as price breaks through the upper trendline of the triangle. The success rate for this trade rises to 94% with a confirmation of volume.

Bearish Symmetrical Triangle Pattern

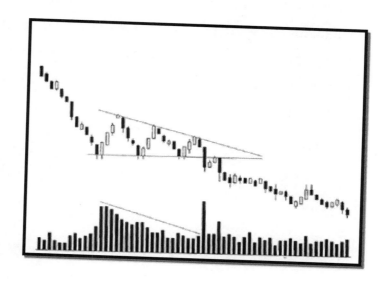

This continuation pattern typically occurs after a large increase in price. After price goes through a consolidation or correction, this chart pattern begins to form with a decrease in volume, while the trend will usually continue in the same direction just before it begins to contract.

Price targets can be calculated by measuring the vertical distance of the open end of the triangle. If you are following an explosive stock, you can always use a trailing stop loss to capture more of the move, depending on your preference.

The drop in volume for this pattern is followed by a huge spike in volume that reveals that sellers are rushing onto the market for this stock. This spike in volume confirms the trade as price breaks through the lower trendline of the triangle. The success rate for this trade rises to 98% with a confirmation of volume.

Double Bottoms & Tops

Double Bottom Pattern

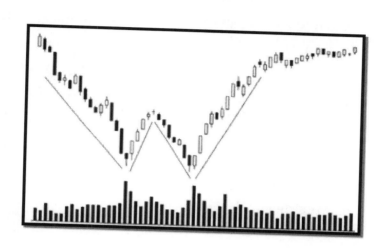

A Double Bottom is a bullish reversal pattern usually occurring after an extended downward move in price. After a reversal at the first bottom accompanied by high volume, momentum will be lost at the confirmation level and price will decline again, resulting in the second bottom. A second reversal will be accompanied again by high volume, and a secondary volume peak will accompany the stock as it breaks above the confirmation level.

I recommend using this pattern in conjunction with the 3

types of trends discussed earlier for superior trend identification. For example, if the dominant trend on the larger timeframe is up while the smaller timeframe is down, you want to watch for this pattern on the smaller timeframe to confirm a resumption of the dominant upward trend.

One more bit of advice: bottoms that occur closer together are stronger than ones timed further apart.

High volume at each bottom reversal with a secondary volume spikes as the pattern "confirms" by breaking above the confirmation level.

By not confirming the breakout after the second bottom, the pattern may just become another bearish channeling pattern, rising and falling between support and resistance.

To trade the pattern effectively, you want to identify the confirmation level and confirm that prices have closed above the price before entering a bullish position. On good double bottom patterns, the second bottom will undercut the first bottom.

The typical success rate for a Double Bottom pattern in and

of itself is pretty lackluster and unremarkable at just 36%. However, if you wait for price to rise above the confirmation level, that success rate skyrockets to a startling 97%, making this one of the most effective trading patterns when confirmed by breakout volume.

Double Top Pattern

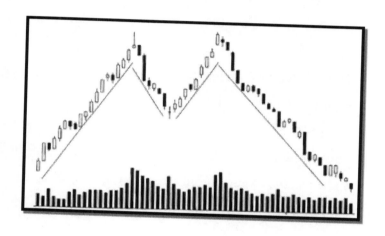

A Double Top is a bearish reversal pattern usually occurring after an extended upward move in price. After a reversal at the first top accompanied by high volume, momentum will be lost at the confirmation level and the price will rise again, resulting in the second top. A second reversal will be accompanied again by high volume, and a secondary volume peak will accompany the stock as it breaks below the confirmation level.

I recommend using this pattern in conjunction with the 3 types of trends discussed earlier for superior trend identification. For example, if the dominant trend on the larger timeframe is down while the smaller timeframe is up, you want to watch for this pattern on the smaller timeframe to confirm a resumption of the dominant downward trend.

One more bit of advice: tops that occur closer together are stronger than ones timed further apart.

High volume at each top reversal with a secondary volume spikes as the pattern "confirms" by breaking below the confirmation level.

By not confirming the breakout after the second top, the pattern may just become another bullish channeling pattern, rising and falling between support and resistance.

To trade the pattern effectively, you want to identify the confirmation level and confirm that prices have closed below that price before entering a bearish position. On

148

good Double Top patterns, the second top will undercut the first top.

The success rate for the Double Top pattern is slightly different than its counterpart, the Double Bottom. The Double Top has a very low 35% success rate when traded off just its price action, but when confirmed, the success rate rises to a very high 83%.

Why is this? It's because calling tops in the markets is always a lot trickier than calling the bottoms. Because of this, you will notice that some bearish patterns have slightly lower success rates than others.

The Wrap-Up

The price patterns detailed above are among the most commonly sighted patterns in the stock market and are among the most reliable when trading.

Remember, price patterns in and of themselves are not a reason to trade a stock or security but to help you gain an understanding of what price is doing and why it is performing the way it is. These two traits help you predict what price is going to do next and, depending on the context, decide whether to buy or sell.

8. Intro to Technical Tools

While the ability to read price action alone can give you a strong competitive edge over many traders, using the right set of technical tools can be of great use as well. Technical tools are a combination of market indicators and gauges that give you the ability to see where the market is oversold/overbought and where the market is likely to resume its trend or reverse its course.

In the following pages, I'm going to detail for you a handful of effective indicators that, if mastered, will help you profitably navigate the market, but I want to address an age-old argument about price action analysis versus indicators first. In my opinion, the ability to read price is more effective than using indicators by themselves. Markets are not traded efficiently, and using indicators created by the same fallible people who also make up the market doesn't seem to very logical to me.

Markets that are trending strongly in a given direction can continue to move in that direction despite oversold/overbought readings by technical indicators. Markets are driven by human emotion, which cannot be

151

factored into a defined set of technical criteria. I am sure that the best minds in the world are working on it, but markets are irrational, just like the human beings that trade them, and therefore price is expressed as wildly as fear, greed, euphoria, and the whole gamut of human emotion.

Traders, especially beginners, are often sucked into the idea that using the latest indicators will tell them when to buy, sell, or hold. To put it bluntly, this is "get rich quick" thinking that rarely, if ever, leads to any meaningful success in trading.

You have to want to be able to make your decisions based on your own critical thinking about what the market is doing in the ever-present *now* and make adjustments based on new information coming in from the market's price movement.

In my own view, indicators and technical tools act as strong secondary measures to help you confirm your own analysis made by reading the actual price action of the market or underlying security.

152

As long as you don't rely on indicators by themselves to make your trade decisions, they can be great tools to help you make better trades.

In the next few pages, I'm going to detail a few of the most common indicators to help guide your trading decisions.

Moving Averages

Moving averages are an indicator in technical analysis that helps smooth out price action by filtering out the "noise" from random price fluctuations. A moving average, or MA, is a trend-following or lagging indicator because it is based on past prices.

One commonly used MA is the simple moving average (SMA), which is the simple average of a security over a defined number of time periods.

The most common application of MAs is identifying the trend direction and determining support and resistance levels. In this book, however, you want to approach the use of MAs in two ways: to give you a visual representation of the current price action in the underlying security, and to help you track what the larger institutional investors are watching.

There are key MAs that large institutional traders and investors watch when they are tracking their own investments or potential investments.

You'll read about these in a moment, but it's important for you to understand why you need to keep an eye on those key MAs. Support and resistance at these MAs are almost a self-fulfilling prophecy as traders react to price touching these levels as well as entry and exit points.

By knowing in advance what the Big Players are looking at and preparing for any reaction to these levels, you have an edge to control your risk as well as to profitably exploit those reactions.

The 10-day Simple Moving Average

A simple moving average (SMA) is formed by adding the price of a security over a specific number of periods and then dividing by the number of periods (like an average price). Moving averages are based on closing prices. For example, a 10-day moving average is the 10-day sum of closing prices divided by 10. As its name implies, a moving average is an average that moves.

This moving average is popular with short-term traders, particularly swing traders and even day traders, because it helps you determine the trend over the last 5 to 10 trading days.

Short-term fluctuations are chaotic, but this MA gives a quick visual reference as to what price movement is in the short-term, which helps you in two ways: you can spot momentum in short-term price action and you can spot low-risk entry/exit points in price.

When a trend is in effect, the "natural order" is for MAs to be stacked on top of each other. For bullish markets, this means that the 10-day SMA will trade above the longer-term MAs like the 50-day and then the 200-day, which you'll read about in more detail in just a while.

For bearish markets, the 10-day SMA will trade below the 50-day, and then both will trade below the 200-day SMA.

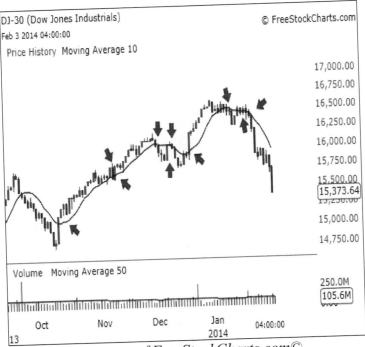

Courtesy of FreeStockCharts.com©
Fig. 1

The arrows show several points in the Dow's price movement where there was potential to ride the index's momentum or exit as price crossed its path.

When all MAs are in that natural order and sloping in a given direction, there is strength, or momentum, in the current price trend. But when momentum is waning, it will

156

first appear in the 10-day SMA and, depending on the context of the market, can signal an entry on a pullback or exit.

The 50-day Simple Moving Average

As night follows day, new bull markets serve up big, new market leaders. Excellent fundamentals and increasing mutual fund ownership are two main catalysts for huge gains for select stocks.

But all good runs eventually come to an end, and this is especially true in the stock market. The fifty-day SMA is a key MA that the big institutional traders follow to help determine when the band is about to stop playing, which is why it's critical for the smart trader to follow it as well.

After a stock's lengthy run-up, it's always important to watch for signs of heavy institutional selling.

For a market leader, the 50-day moving average, which computes a running average of price closes over the past fifty trading sessions, can act as a support level during an uptrend. But it can also act as a resistance level during a downtrend.

If a stock breaks below the fifty-day line in heavy volume and can't rally back, this is often a signal that buying demand is drying up and the stock's run is ending. Keep in mind that one or two bursts of institutional selling can often presage more sales ahead. Sometimes, it can take a fund several weeks to exit a position.

Studying the price action of former market leaders just before they broke down can help you act quickly when a current leader you own starts to falter.

The fifty-day SMA is a line that can act as either support or resistance.

Support - Let's say we're looking at a company whose stock price has been increasing for some time and hasn't touched the 50-day SMA in months but then begins to decline. Price is falling fast, and it looks like it's just going to slice through its 50-day SMA, but as soon as it makes contact, price bounces off and begins to resume its trend. Why? Because many traders will either buy into the stock or add to an existing position at the 50-day SMA, where it finds the necessary support to continue its bullish trend.

Resistance - If a stock has been trading below its 50 SMA for some time and then starts to trend back upwards, the 50 SMA is normally a point of resistance. This is due to its wide spread use and placement on charts. For technical traders, it gives them an easy target to sell into this new strength or even short the stock.

As you start to watch stocks and look at more charts, take note of this type of technical setup. It is extremely important, because whenever a stock trades at or around this line, you'll see institutional traders use the 50-day SMA as a buy or sell signal that you can exploit for an easy setup.

Fig. 2
The 50-day SMA

Big Daddy: The 200-day Simple Moving Average

The 200-day SMA is a long-term moving average that helps determine the overall health of a stock. The percentage of stocks above their 200-day SMA helps determine the overall health of the market. When this number gets below

20%, many traders look for a sharp reversal in the market that can quickly bring the number up to 40%. When this number gets above 85% or 90%, many traders look for a reversal in the market.

A stock that is trading below its 200-day SMA is in a long-term downtrend. The stock is generally considered unhealthy until it breaks out above its 200-day moving average. Some traders like to buy when a stock's 50 day moving average crosses above its 200-day moving average.

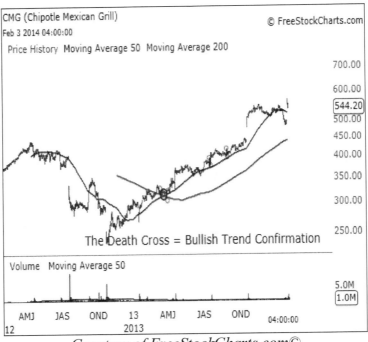

CMG (Chipotle Mexican Grill)
Feb 3 2014 04:00:00

Price History Moving Average 50 Moving Average 200

© FreeStockCharts.com

700.00
600.00
544.20
500.00
450.00
400.00
350.00
300.00
250.00

The Death Cross = Bullish Trend Confirmation

Volume Moving Average 50

5.0M
1.0M

AMJ   JAS   OND   13   AMJ   JAS   OND   04:00:00
12   2013

Courtesy of FreeStockCharts.com©

Fig. 3

The Death Cross occurs when the 50-day SMA crosses through the 200-day SMA and indicates that one side—bulls or bears—is taking control of price.

A stock that is trading above its 200-day SMA is in a long-term uptrend. This is considered a healthy indication. A healthy stock will generally have a rising 200-day SMA. When its 50 day moving average crosses below its 200-day SMA, this is called a Death Cross.

The 200-day SMA often works as a major support level in a bull market. This can present a low-risk opportunity to buy

162

a stock, however a break below it can lead to a large gap downward. In a bear market, the 200-day SMA often works as a major resistance level; however, a break above it can lead to a sharp rise.

In a bull market, a buying signal may be generated as the stock dips close to the 200-day SMA, and a sell signal may be generated when it goes far above its 200-day SMA. In a bear market, a buying signal may be generated when it dips far below its 200-day SMA, and a sell signal may be generated when it rises close to its 200-day SMA. However, the opposite signals may be generated on strong breakthroughs of the 200-day SMA.

The 200-day SMA is a popular, quantified long-term trend indicator.

Markets trading above the 200-day SMA tend to be in longer-term uptrends. Markets trading below the 200-day SMA tend to be in longer-term downtrends.

Larry Connors, in his book *Short Term Trading Strategies That Work: A Quantified Guide to Trading Stocks and ETFs*, writes:

"As a general rule, many people like to buy stocks when they've been beaten down over a long period of time. You'll see people "bottom-fishing" stocks as they are plunging lower under their 200-day moving average however once a stock drops under its 200-day moving average, you're better off buying stocks in a longer term uptrend than in a longer term down trend."

On-Balance Indicator

The On-Balance Indicator, or OBV, is used to detect momentum, the calculation of which relates volume to price change. The OBV provides a running total of volume and shows whether this volume is flowing in or out of a given security.

The OBV attempts to detect when a financial instrument is being accumulated by a large number of buyers or sold by many sellers. Traders will use an upward-sloping OBV to confirm an uptrend, while a downward-sloping OBV is used to confirm a downtrend. Finding a downward-sloping OBV while the price of an asset is trending upward suggests that the "smart" traders are starting to exit their positions and that a shift in trend may be coming.

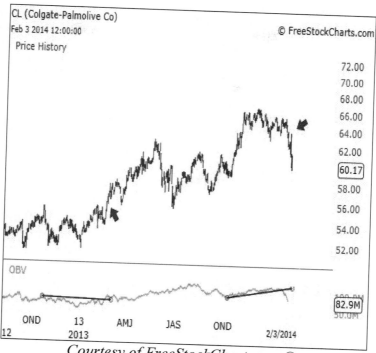

Fig. 4

The OBV indicator shows where accumulation and distribution is taking place in a stock. Here, CL rises as accumulation takes place at the arrow on the left just as the OBV begins to break higher which shows accumulation. On the right side of the chart, the upward trendline of the OBV indicator breaks lower, showing distribution in CL just as the stock begins to decline.

Bollinger Bands

Bollinger Bands consist of a center line with two price channels above and below it. The center line is an exponential moving average; the price channels are the standard deviations of the stock being studied. The bands will expand and contract as the price action of an issue becomes volatile (expansion) or becomes bound into a tight trading pattern (contraction).

Standard deviation is a mathematical concept that measures volatility, showing how stock price can vary from its true value. By measuring price volatility, Bollinger bands adjust themselves to market conditions. This is what makes them so handy for traders: traders can find almost the entire price data needed between the two bands.

When stock prices continually touch the upper Bollinger Band, the prices are thought to be overbought; conversely, when they continually touch the lower band, prices are thought to be oversold, triggering a buy signal.

166

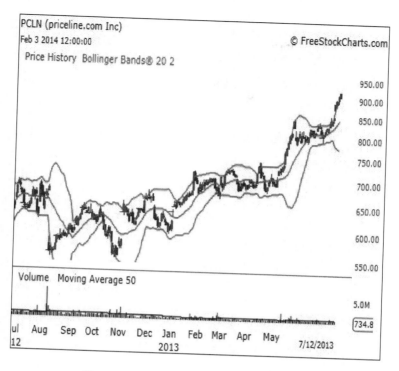

PCLN (priceline.com Inc)
Feb 3 2014 12:00:00
© FreeStockCharts.com
Price History Bollinger Bands® 20 2

950.00
900.00
850.00
800.00
750.00
700.00
650.00
600.00
550.00

Volume   Moving Average 50

5.0M
734.8

ul Aug Sep Oct Nov Dec Jan Feb Mar Apr May
12   2013   7/12/2013

Courtesy of FreeStockCharts.com©
Fig. 5

Bollinger Bands act as a visual reference showing where a stock's price action is trading in relation to its historical volatility. Notice how they act as support and resistance to PCLN's price action even as the stock trends higher. These act as reliable entry and exit points for trading.

When using Bollinger Band, you can designate the upper and lower bands as price targets. If the price deflects off the lower band and crosses above the 20-day average center line, the upper band comes to represent the upper price target. In a strong uptrend, prices usually fluctuate between the upper band and the 20-day moving average. When that happens, a crossing below the 20-day moving average can serve as a warning of a trend reversal to the downside.

This is also an excellent indicator for price contraction in any underlying security's price action that you may be tracking.

Low volatility tends to follow high volatility, and vice versa. During periods of price contraction, volatility tends to fall and can be spotted easily when the Bollinger Bands tighten their trading range. Since volatility tends to revert to its mean by returning from a low-volatility environment to a high-volatility environment, you can gain a competitive edge over other traders by taking note of where low-volatile price action is taking place and exploiting price when it returns to a high-volatile environment where price moves out of contraction and into expansion once again.

On the other side of the coin, when price is highly volatile and trading beyond the range of the Bollinger Bands, you can expect volatility to return to its mean where high volatility is followed by low volatility. This sets the stage

168

for a price reversal where price moves from expansion to contraction, usually from a price trend to a trading range.

Keltner Channels

This indicator, named after Chester W. Keltner, is used by sophisticated investors to predict the trend of the market. An overbought condition occurs when prices move above the upper band, and an oversold condition occurs when prices move below the lower band.

The Keltner channel is a volatility-based "envelope" indicator that measures the movement of stocks in relation to an upper and lower moving-average band. As a result, this volatility-based technical indicator bears many similarities to the Bollinger Bands. The difference between the two studies is simply that Keltner's channels represent volatility using the high and low prices, while Bollinger's studies rely on the standard deviation. Like Bollinger Bands, Keltner channel signals are produced when the price action breaks above or below the channel bands.

Fig. 6

Keltner channels create bands similar to Bollinger bands
but with a slight variation. Keltner channels use the price
of the stock, whereas Bollinger bands use standard
deviation. Both offer good guides as to where support and
resistance can be found in a stock's price chart as well as
where price trades at extremes for price reversals.

9. Simple Stock Trading Formulas

In the following pages, you'll read about several different trading formulas that can be used for reliable results in your trading. They have been time-tested and battle-proven.

Keep in mind that they have to be used in the context of what price action is doing and in relation to sound technical analysis and trend identification. If you use the tools you've learned up to this point, that shouldn't be a problem for you.

The nice thing about these trading formulas is that they are standalone methods but can be used in conjunction with one another for spectacular results.

Take your time learning them and be patient with yourself, and you'll be happy with the results that follow.

9.1. The 100 S/R Trend Trading Formula

100 S/R Trend Trading Formula

The logic behind this trade setup is that the trend is revealed at a glance using a simple filter, the 100 SMA, while the entries are focused on key areas of support/resistance. Trading trends this way lets you enter into a move that gets underway at one of the lowest risk points before the resumption of the trend.

Using a 100-day SMA on a price chart, the following rules for this setup:

For longs.

1. 100-day Simple Moving Average (SMA) is trending upward.

2. Price is above the 100 SMA.

3. Price declines to make a significant low.

4. Price rises from that significant low price point and then retests that low no less than 10 days later.

5. Enter on the close of the first bar that closes above the price bar that retested the prior significant low point.

Courtesy of FreeStockCharts.com©

Fig. 1

The 100 SMA is trending upward when on 11-29-2013 a price low is set followed by a retest of that support level on 12-16-2013 and a setup condition has been met. The day after that retest, on 12-17-13, price closes above the intraday high of the previous day, which signals a long *entry at $52.22. Price has traded as high as $62.75 in less than two months, a gain of over ten points or just over 20%.*

For shorts.

1. 100-day Simple Moving Average (SMA) is trending downward.

2. Price is below the 100-day SMA.

3. Price rallies to make a significant high.

4. Price declines from that significant high price point and then retests that high no less than ten days later.

5. Enter on the close of the first bar that closes below the price bar that retested the prior significant high point.

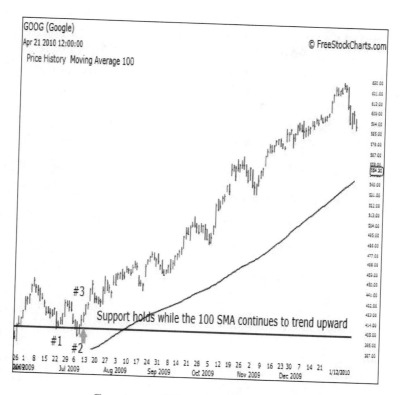

Courtesy of FreeStockCharts.com©

Fig. 2

Google (GOOG) also offered a setup using this method on 6-22-09 (Figure 3) when price declined to set a low at $401.89 at Point #1 while the 100 SMA was trending upward.

At Point #2, 10 trading days later on 7-07-09, price declined to test the previous low. Two days later, on 7-09-09, an entry was triggered (Point #3) at $410.39.

GOOG goes on to trend as high as $629.41 on 1-04-10 before seriously declining, but not before offering a potential gain of $219.02, or 53%, in just five months.

The logic behind this trade setup is that the trend is revealed at a glance using a simple filter, the 100-day SMA, while the entries are focused on key areas of support/resistance. Trading trends this way lets you enter into a move that gets underway at one of the lowest risk points just before a resumption of the trend.

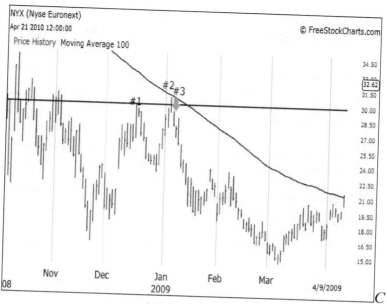

ourtesy of FreeStockCharts.com©

Fig. 3

A price high is set at Point #1 followed by a restest of resistance at Point #2 thirteen days later. NYX rallies back to test this high on 1-06-09, and on the following day, 1/07/09, an entry is signaled at Point #3 when price closes below the previous price bar's high at $27.93.

NYX went on to decline to a low of $14.52 on 3-06-09, where you could have covered the short for a potential gain of $13.41, or 48%, in two months.

Support and resistance lines have been one of the most reliable price patterns for stock traders because they offer a quantified price point for entry. When price reaches a significant low or high and then comes back to retest that low or high, this indicates the resumption of the primary trend.

Because of their high reliability, many traders trade these areas almost exclusively. When combined with a simple indicator, their effectiveness can be leveraged into a much bigger potential trade.

9.2. The Rattlesnake Volatility Formula

Price & Volatility

If you've been trading for any length of time, you probably realize that for every time a stock is trending, there will be later periods when that stock will be stuck in a price range. As price action experiences expansion by trending either upwards or downwards, it will settle into a consolidation period and form a trading range or, over time, a price pattern.

But floor traders can see the same price patterns as you do and bid up the price of a stock to give the appearance that a breakout move is underway in order to draw in off-the-floor traders and then cash out as new buy orders enter the market. As floor traders sell into the buying frenzy, support for the new price levels inevitably falls, and then they can turn around to short the market as price declines.

Floor traders manipulate the markets more frequently than many would like to admit, and this has been going on for a very long time.

This leads to the next question: "How do I identify these contracted price ranges and then time my trade with the highest probability of success?"

The answer is to use a few simple technical indicators to help you identify the ideal set of conditions for an explosive move while also helping you gain an edge on timing your entry.

Rattlesnake Volatility Formula

All over the Southwest of the United States, rattlesnakes are commonplace, and when the snake feels threatened it will begin to shake the end of its tail, creating a rattling sound.

In much the same way, the Rattlesnake Volatility Formula will alert you when the market is coiled up and ready to strike in advance of the actual move.

The steps of the rattlesnake volatility formula are:

1) Overlay Bollinger Bands on a price chart with a 20 period, 2 standard-deviation setting.

180

2) Overlay Keltner Channels on the price chart with the Bollinger Bands, but set a 20-period setting.

3) At the bottom of the chart, input the Chaikin Oscillator to monitor the flow of money in and out of the the stock and set at a 21-period setting.

For Longs:

1) The Bollinger Bands constrict within the lines of the Keltner Channel, indicating price contraction within the trading range (snake coil), and the Chaikin Oscillator is below the zero baseline.

2) When the Chaikin oscillator passes back up through the zero baseline, this indicates that the stock is under accumulation and you should go long (the "rattle" indicating that an upside breakout move is about to happen).

For Shorts:

1) The Bollinger Bands constrict within the lines of the Keltner Channel, indicating price contraction within the trading range (snake coil), and the Chaikin Oscillator is above the zero baseline.

2) When the Chaikin Oscillator passes back down through the zero baseline, this indicates that the stock is under distribution and you should go short (the "rattle" that a downside breakout move is about to happen).

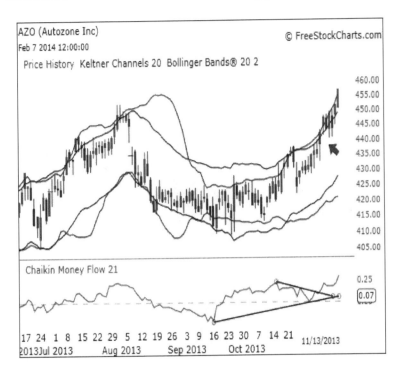

Courtesy of FreeStockCharts.com©

Figure 1

AutoZone (AZO) begins to contract into a tight trading range where the Rattlesnake Volatility Formula begins to setup when the Bollinger Bands trade within the Keltner Channels in September of 2013. The Chaikin indicator begins to rise up through the zero-line and trend higher, *mimicking AZO's price action. On November 5th, 2013, price rises up through a buy point of $437.50 just as the Bollinger Bands expand outside of the Keltner Channels, indicating that volatility is expanding along with price.*

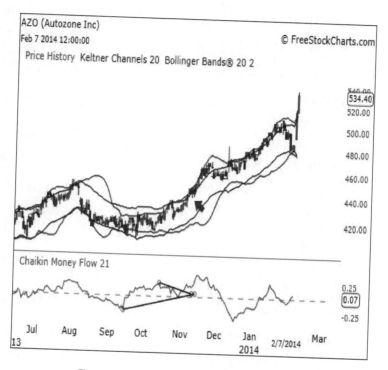

Courtesy of FreeStockCharts.com©

Figure 2

AZO gains almost 97 points for a potential 22% gain in just 4 months with lots of upside potential remaining.

183

Important Details

The Bollinger Bands are a moving average based on the volatility of a stock while the Keltner Channels act as a moving average of the price high, low, and close of the stock. When the Bollinger Bands contracts between the Keltner Channels, this reveals that there is a reduction in volatility.

Because volatility reverts to its mean and lower volatility is followed by higher volatility, there is potential for price to explode out of its current state into a period of price expansion. All that is needed is a trigger to act as the catalyst.

The catalyst for this move is unveiled in the Chaikin oscillator. As a match acts as the catalyst to release the potential power of inert dynamite, so acts the accumulation or distribution indicated by the Chaikin to release the potential breakout power of a stock in a contracted price range.

9.3. The Juggernaut Surge Formula

So far, a lot has been written about stocks that have strong fundamentals for good candidates to find compelling technical criteria that can translate into high-probability trade setups. This is for good reason, since most high-performing stocks tend to trend and show strength. But this doesn't account for stocks that lack fundamentals lack institutional sponsorship that go on to make spectacular runs in their price action.

At times, there are stocks that have no apparent reason to perform well that end up making breathtaking run-ups in price that rack up 100% to 1,000% returns or more in short periods of time. Sometimes the reasons are apparent only after the move has begun or right as the run-up seems to end, but, sadly, many traders miss these moves by being unprepared.

The reason most traders miss out on these types of surges in price is that they don't have a framework to help identify them before they break higher. In this chapter, you're going to learn about a framework to help identify these types of moves as they are gathering strength and how to latch onto their move as they soar higher with seemingly unstoppable strength.

The Juggernaut Surge Formula

When a stock accelerates in value in a short period of time, the stock's price action is like an unstoppable juggernaut that marches forward regardless of what is going on in the market or the global economy.

The rules for this method are elegant in their simplicity but powerful in their application.

They are:

1) Watch for any stock that makes a 50% increase in price within an 8 week period.

2) The stock must have a 20-day average volume level of 100,000 shares traded daily at the time of entry.

3) Enter on the next available price high as price climbs higher.

When you see a stock setting up with a huge price surge, you don't need to emphasize what the stock's fundamentals are or what the broader market is experiencing.

The juggernaut surge is a pure play on price action, so you don't need any qualifier other than the stock's surge in price within an eight-week period.

Example: Priceline (PCLN)

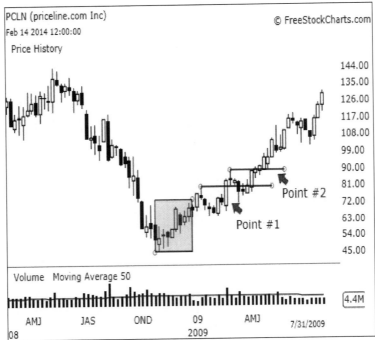

Courtesy of FreeStockCharts.com ©
Figure 1

Priceline (PCLN) had been a high-performing stock up until the housing crisis of 2008 came to a full boil and spilled over into the stock market as a whole. As a result, the toxic housing assets that caused the crash took down every other stock, not just housing stocks, and PCLN got caught up in the decline.

188

In Figure 1, you can see on PCLN's weekly price chart that price declined from $144 to a price low of just under $47 a share. But as soon as PCLN hit its bottom, its stock gathered strength and gained a quick 50%-plus gain in just under eight weeks. The setup for a condition had been met, and it was a matter of patience to see when the opportunity presented itself to pull the trigger and go long.

About three weeks later, price pulled back briefly and then began to resume its trend once again. A buy entry was signaled at Point #1, just over the $80 price point, in February of 2009.

It would have been advisable to set your stop just under the previous low at $65.10 and then trail that stop loss point as the stock climbed higher.

Price did pull back shortly after the entry at Point #1 but then offered a second entry at Point #2 as a result. This could have been a second chance to enter the move if you missed the initial entry or a chance to add to your existing position.

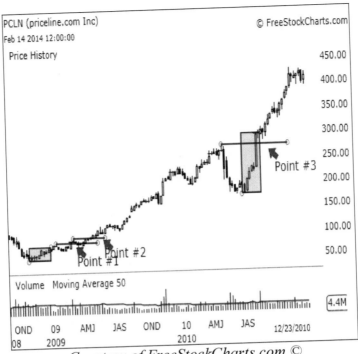

Courtesy of FreeStockCharts.com ©

Figure 2

PCLN continued to rise from both entry points and make significant gains to as high as $273.94 a share (see Fig. 2). From an original entry point of $80, and with you trailing your stop loss under each new price low along the way, you could potentially have almost two hundred points before PCLN experienced a significant pullback in April of 2010.

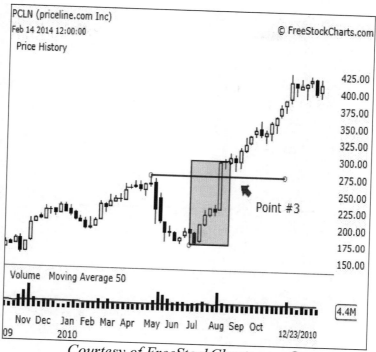

Point #3

Courtesy of FreeStockCharts.com ©

Figure 3

But PCLN's move wasn't done.

In June of 2010, just a few months later, PCLN bottomed out at $184.01 and then surged greater than 50% within another 8 week timeframe (see Fig. 3).

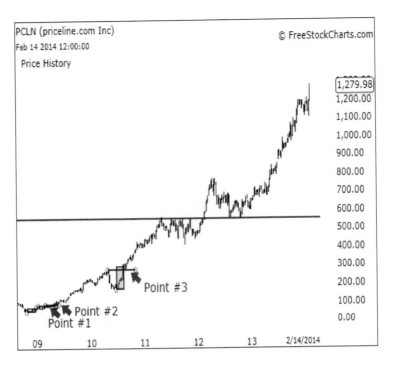

Courtesy of FreeStockCharts.com ©
Figure 4

A long entry was signaled at the beginning of August 2010 just under $274 right as PCLN was picking up steam to trade higher.

PCLN went on to trade at up to $561 a share before experiencing a correction (see Fig. 4) in May of 2011 for a potential gain of 284 points translating, into a 100% gain in just 9 months.

However, if you kept a wide stop loss order to hang onto a position, the stock is now trading at just over $1,280 a share for a potential windfall of over 500% in less than 3½ years.

This pattern plays out over and over again in the stock market. You just have to remain alert and watch for quick accelerations in price made by any stock with adequate volume in order to remain liquid.

Catching just one or two of these moves each year would give you an annual average that any professional money manager would drool over, so put in the time to learn how to use this formula to spot these stocks just before they take off.

9.4. The Insider Trading Formula

Inside Price Action

"Inside Bars" is a term used by traders to label a price bar where the high point of the price bar is lower than the previous day's high and the low point is higher than the previous day's low. Inside bars reveal reduced volatility in an underlying security that is transitioning into a period of contraction. This is common when an underlying security has experienced a sustained trend and is then followed by a reversal from its previous direction.

194

Courtesy of FreeStockCharts.com ©

Figure 1

Ichan Enterprises Lp (IEP) formed a Triangle Chart Pattern in late 2013 that broke out on 9-9-13, but a better entry presented itself when IEP pulled back and formed an inside bar on 10-9-13. A long entry was signaled the next day at $83.71 as price resumed its upward move and traded as high as $148 on 12-9-13 before a price correction took place.

Pull up a price chart and you'll see price sprinkled with Inside Bars that trade within the previous trading day's price range and are typically followed by reversals in that price movement. Inside bars reveal points in price where the ascent/descent of price action is in question because traders who are participating in that underlying security's movement are at an impasse about whether to continue on course and stay put or exit altogether.

This indecision results in the formation of the price pattern until either the bulls or the bears enter in sufficient number to take control of the trend.

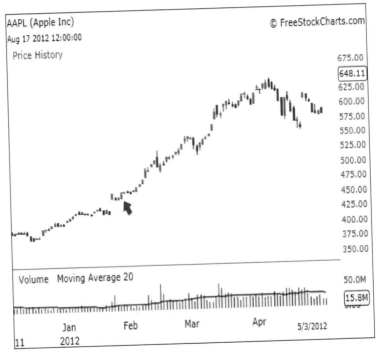

Courtesy of FreeStockCharts.com ©

Figure 2

196

On 1-25-12, AAPL exploded upward on huge volume, forming a large price gap, and within a couple days formed an Inside Price Bar on 1-27-12 followed by a low-risk entry the following day at $448.58. Just 4 months later, AAPL peaked at almost 200 points higher with an initial risk of only four points at the time of entry.

Multi-Inside Price Bars is a phenomenon that occurs when neither side—bulls nor bears—has managed to take control of the trend, with price meandering back and forth after a strong run-up or decline. Similar to trading price channels, look for price to break out of this range in the direction of the primary trend. A price reversal can give you a tremendous edge in spotting the upcoming price movement.

Inside bars can be used to enter into confirmed price trends or in trading off support and resistance levels depending on the context of the market.

For example, one of the most common complaints about breakout trading is that the moves are so explosive that they can catch you unaware, and, before you realize it, the entry point has escaped you. However, by using inside bars, you can enjoy the benefits of breakout trading with better entry points.

Once price begins to pull back, any inside bar formed during the brief pullback will make a compelling entry point for the skilled trader. A long entry over the high of the inside bar in a bullish market and a short entry below the low of the inside bar for a bearish market are reliable entry approaches when using this price pattern to profit during strong trends.

Trading support/resistance levels is a staple for most traders, and since the price zones are clearly defined they offer high-probability trades using inside bars.

Once you observe that an inside bar has formed at a particular price level, you wait for an entry above or below the inside price bar, depending on the context of the setup. The forming of such a price pattern at a defined price zone—support or resistance—reveals that price is likely to reverse from that particular level and change course. An entry at the upper level of the inside bar off a support level for a bullish trade and an entry below the low of the inside bar off the resistance level for a bearish trade.

The Sushi Roll

Inside price bars, in and of themselves, can be for trading trends or support/resistance, but they can also be used in combinations to spot powerful price reversals.

198

One of these patterns is the "Sushi Roll" pattern, discovered by Mark Fisher, trader and author of the book *The Logical Trader*, during lunch one day when discussing trade setups and their use with his colleagues.

The major benefit of this pattern is that it signals a potential price reversal much sooner than chart patterns like a Double Bottom or Head & Shoulders, for example. It's also applicable to any timeframe, so it can be customized depending on your own trading preferences.

However, it is important to note that the ten-price bar rule is not set in stone. What is important is the underlying principle that any price range that trades in a small trading range followed by price action that engulfs that trading range indicates a strong case for a price reversal. This knowledge alone can help you avoid unnecessary losses by tightening up your stops, taking profits, or exiting the trade altogether.

The strategy can be modified on larger timeframes by conservative traders simply by increasing the number of days to watch for using the pattern's underlying principles. Increasing the days counted to as much as twenty, for example, can help you avoid false moves better compared to using the ten-day pattern. You sacrifice getting into a market reversal earlier and lose some of the early profit potential, but the trade-off is that you can catch trends that have the potential for lasting for years by taking into account the larger timeframe.

Courtesy of FreeStockCharts.com ©

Figure 3

On the weekly timeframe, the SPX traded downward from early January 2009 to mid-March of the same year (see #1), followed by narrow price action that traded within the previous downward price range. Using a ten-period range from the price low set in January, the SPX traded within the previous price range until thirteen weeks later when it took out the high of the previous trading range, reversing the trend to hand control back to the bulls.

9.5. The Game Changer Formula

Price reversals can be a brutal and shocking game-changer. Complacent hedge fund managers and professional traders have been off-guard and wiped out as a result of price reversals.

Any trend, no matter how strong it is or how long it has been in place, can outrun its underlying fundamentals or changing technical criteria. Like a rubber band that has been stretched to its limit, at some point it will snap back in the opposite direction.

In a fast-moving market, not knowing when price reversal will appear is like playing Russian roulette. Even if you get lucky five times, the one time the gun's cylinder rotates a live round in front of the falling hammer, you are through.

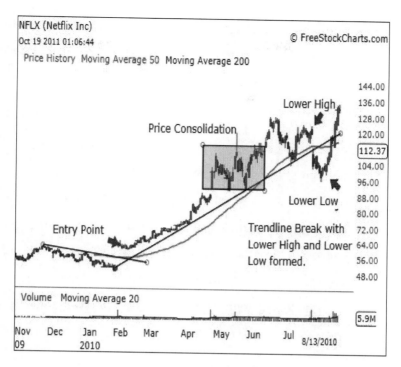

Courtesy of FreeStockCharts.com©
Fig. 1

NFLX rocketed higher from its breakout and consolidated in price from early April of 2010 to June of the same year. No lower-highs or lower-lows appeared during that consolidation period, revealing that the bullish trend was not intact until it experienced a mild price reversal on 7-22-10, when the trend line was broken and price went on to form a lower-high by failing to follow through to the upside. This signaled an exit but later offered a second entry on August 12th, 2010 at around $128, resuming its upward trend.

Countless traders fall victim to price reversals, either simply due to the inability to read the warning signs and make adjustments or because they can't read price action accurately.

New trends begin to form depending on whether the underlying security is under active accumulation or distribution. Accumulation occurs when a stock or commodity is being acquired by a sufficient number of investors where the security involved will reflect a gradual increase in price due to rising demand for the security, which makes a steady series of higher-highs and higher-lows.

Distribution occurs when a stock or commodity is being sold while a sufficient number of investors liquidate their holdings to take profits, which results in a gradual price decline as demand for the security falls, resulting in a steady succession of lower-highs and lower-lows in the price action.

If price is not exhibiting either of these behaviors—upward movement or downward movement—then it is consolidating in a trading range until an imbalance in either supply and demand is created, and it will remain in consolidation until either the bulls or the bears gain control and force a trend to emerge.

The game-changer, then, is where an external force, or catalyst, enters the market and changes the dynamic of the direction of the trend, which will be revealed in the trend's price action.

The Game Changer Formula's Rules

The following rules act as a guideline to define the terms or conditions that make a price reversal likely to appear:

1. Select the time period you are trading in and identify the timeframe that the trend is in.

2. Quantify the direction of that trend by drawing a trend line from key price levels.

3. Identify the price breaking through that trend line and fail to follow through.

First, define the time period you are trading in and identify the timeframe that the trend is moving in. For example, if you are holding positions over a period of days to weeks, you are trading an intermediate-term trend and won't need to track the price movement on the short-term or long-term timeframes.

Second, draw a trend line on that timeframe to quantify the trend in place. For bullish trends, you want to draw a trend line from the lowest low point in its price action to the highest low point.

For bearish trends, draw a trend line from the highest low point in its price action to its lowest high point.

Finally, if price breaks through the trend line that defines the current trend and then fails to make a new high if it's a bullish trend or a new low if it's a bearish trend, then the reversal is confirmed.

Price consolidation does not warrant any type of defensive action unless price begins to make contrary high or low points in the price's opposite direction. This type of price action will trade back and forth between two relatively easily identifiable price points where you can draw two horizontal lines between them until one side—bulls or bears—gains the upper hand and takes control of the trend.

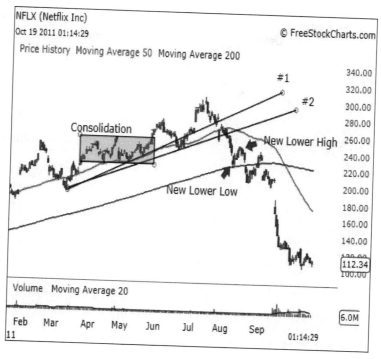

The chart contains the following labels: NFLX (Netflix Inc), Oct 19 2011 01:14:29, © FreeStockCharts.com, Price History Moving Average 50 Moving Average 200, #1, #2, Consolidation, New Lower High, New Lower Low, Volume Moving Average 20, Feb 11, Mar, Apr, May, Jun, Jul, Aug, Sep, price levels 340.00 down to 100.00, 112.34, 6.0M.

Courtesy of FreeStockCharts.com©

Fig. 2

NFLX consolidated in price from late March of 2011 to early June of 2011 before trending higher but falling below Point #1 in mid-June without forming a lower-high or lower-low. On 7-26-11, the price again broke below the upward trend line at Point #2 but formed a lower-high on 8-12-11. This breaking of the trend line with a failure on the part of price to go on and make a higher-high confirmed a price reversal and signaled that a possible new trend may have been emerging. If you had held onto your entire position from the second entry of $128 to this signal to exit at around $221, you're profit potential would have been ninety-three points a share or just under a 73% return.

207

However, just as Netflix's price action signaled an exit, it also indicated the potential for a new trend to emerge when lower-highs and lower-lows were formed. Price then offered two relatively easy entries as it broke through its two-hundred-day SMA and pulled back on 8-31-11 and 9-7-11. In either case, you could have shorted the stock of bought-put options for a directional move to the downside.

Once bullish price action breaks its trendline and fails to follow through, the corresponding price movement will reveal whether a new trend is emerging or whether it's simply a correction through reversing course and forming a series of lower-highs and lower-lows. Likewise, if bearish price action fails to follow through after a break of its downward trendline and begins a series of higher-highs and higher-lows, a reversal to the upside is in play.

Your trendline acts as a static defense point that signals your next course of action in the event that a reversal is taking place. Price, then, dictates your next move in the form of dynamic offense to trade the other way if price signals that movement is moving in the other direction.

Once a trend reversal is validated, you have to take defensive measures because of the likelihood that the current trend will end. The method of doing this is beyond

208

the scope of this chapter, but in such a scenario, you could sell off your position, scale out, tighten your stops, hedge your position using options, or take any other action to protect your trading capital while locking in profits where possible.

Always remember that the market can take your punches longer than you can remain solvent.

The key lesson is that you want to let price dictate what you do next by being an interpreter of price in the present moment, not a predictor of what will come to pass. Using this trading formula will serve as a guide to your trading decisions when the opportunity presents itself as detailed above.

10. Your Game Plan

This chapter will conclude our look at stock-picking by highlighting the best practices individual traders can use to beat Wall Street. It will conclude by looking at Netflix (NFLX) as a case study of good individual trading.

I want to wrap up with a few miscellaneous thoughts on trading with some hard-earned wisdom that I'd like to share with you.

Before I do, keep in mind that trading is like any vocation—the attainment of excellence is a matter of committing to it every day.

Dreams are precious things and are kept safe by dedicated effort and the consistent application of strategies/formulas that are proven to work.

Being a successful stock trader is as much about having a good strategy as it is about doing great research or having great insight. People should understand that they are not Wall Street analysts. This has three huge advantages that should be exploited and one big disadvantage that should be minimized.

Advantages for Individual Traders that Should Be Leveraged

1. Longer time horizon. Whereas mutual funds are judged on a quarterly basis and may face pressure to "follow the herd," individual traders can trade for the long term. Individual traders can take advantage of this by purchasing "boring" companies that are selling for relatively low valuations and waiting for a news catalyst to come along and force them to move up. If you want to use this kind of strategy, one approach is to screen for companies that have lower P/E, P/B, and FCF yields than the overall stock market, an ROE that is consistently above 15%, and a performance over the past year that is at or above the level of the overall market. High-growth "story stocks" that are promoted by the talking heads on TV are likely to be "follow the herd" stories that can offer price trends you can capitalize on, but remember that these types of stocks tend to end badly, so always use stops.

2. Opportunities in small-caps. Huge mutual funds with billions of dollars to invest have trouble investing in small companies due to ownership limitations and trading practicalities. For instance, imagine that a $4 billion mutual fund wants to invest 1% of its assets into a company in order to build a somewhat meaningful position. This means that $40 million is the smallest position size it can take in a company. Mutual funds are generally not allowed to own more than 10% of the outstanding shares of a company, so this is already limiting the universe to $400 million market caps and above. Even at this level, buying up 10% of all the outstanding shares is time-consuming and likely to push the price up a lot in the process. Be careful to do your homework first: just because a company is small does not mean that its share price is going to go up. If you are interested in taking this kind of approach, it is advantageous to either do really thorough research on your own or to manage a diversified portfolio of twenty or more small stocks so that if a single purchase "blows up" it will not destroy the performance of your overall portfolio.

3. Better insight on "Main Street" trends. A third advantage that is too frequently ignored is that individual traders may actually know some companies and trends better than the Wall Street analysts that cover them. Wall Street can sometimes be out of touch with "Main Street" trends (how many friends of millionaire portfolio managers do you think eat at Chipotle, shop at Wal-Mart, etc.). Stock traders can leverage this to their advantage by investing in companies they know and love. Keep an eye out for new trends. Buy companies you know and like that seem to be catching on with your friends (of course, make sure not to pay too much for them by checking various valuation ratios).

Disadvantage for individual traders that should be minimized.

The major disadvantage of being an individual trader is that you do not have as much time to thoroughly research companies and you do not have the access to company management and other resources that the big players do. So "don't fight the tape." Large institutional investors that catch on to a fundamental development will affect the price when they try to move into or out of a position, thereby telegraphing that they have changed their view.

Follow these four rules - *Pay attention to both fundamental and technical criteria, look at smaller stocks for opportunities, look for price trends, and don't fight the tape. Follow these rules and you will likely have a good chance of beating Wall Street at its own game.*

Netflix (NFLX) as a final case study

NFLX is a wonderfully instructive stock for a number of reasons. Millions of Americans were happy users of the service back in 2007, 2008, and 2009 when the shares were trading at between $20 and $40. These traders had all the data they needed to make a stock purchase that would go up to over ten times their original value over the next few years. They knew that they were happy users of the service, they knew that their friends were happy users of the service, and they knew that the service had the chance to really spread virally. Moreover, the stock price did not seem to already incorporate this information.

A look at the 2008 Netflix annual report shows a net income of $83 million and 9.39 million subscribers on revenue of $1.3 billion, while the market capitalization at the time was above $1.5 billion on a $30 share price. Thus, NFLX was trading at around an 18 P/E multiple and 1.1 P/S multiple on the previous year's sales. None of this seems extraordinarily high for a company with extremely positive fundamentals and the possibility of exponential growth into the future. Earnings growth had been strong even in a very weak economy—earnings grew by over 20% in 2008 and were expected to continue to grow at a double-digit clip, putting the PEG ratio below 1. NFLX's streaming service seemed to be taking off, so it was easy to see the subscriber base doubling or tripling in the next few years as more people found out about the convenience of the service. Moreover, the stock had started to recover impressively

214

from its 2008 lows, so there was strong evidence that Wall Street investors were beginning to get interested in the story. In short, all the necessary ingredients for an individual investor to purchase NFLX shares in early 2009 for a price between $25 and $40 a share were there.

Over the next few years, the stock would go up more than seven times its price to a high of $300 a share.

Of course, at some point this story became less about the fundamentals and more about the momentum. NFLX was mentioned seemingly every day by the financial sites, the P/E went from under 20 to more than 80 at its peak (even though earnings doubled in two years), and the stock was increasingly supported by momentum purchasers. So in 2011 when NFLX announced that it was raising prices in order to pass along increased content costs, there was a rush of momentum money out the door and the stock was dramatically cut from around $300 a share to $110 a share. Whether it is a good buy or not today depends on your view of the streaming industry going forward. But at a purchase price of around $30 in 2009, NFLX would have paid off very handsomely in either case provided you had criteria to identify the opportunity and a method to act as a guide for your trading decisions.

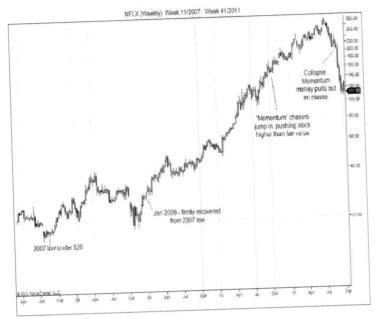

NFLX (Weekly) Week 11/2007 Week 41/2011

Collapse.
Momentum
money pulls out
en masse.

"Momentum" chasers
jump in, pushing stock
higher than fair value

Jan 2009 - firmly recovered
from 2007 low

2007 low under $20

Price chart by NinjaTrader©

10.1. 10 Important Questions You Need to Ask

Questions to ask when analyzing a business

Business

- How does the company make money?

- Does it seem like it should be a good business? Is it competitive? Do suppliers have too much power? Do customers value the product? Are there substitutes?

- Without looking at financials, how does the company seem like it has done against competitors in its industry in terms of executing on its vision?

- What reputation does the management team have? Do they seem honest? Straightforward?

Valuation

- What is the company's P/E multiple? Is it high or low for its industry? For the overall market right now? Why might the stock be trading at this valuation?

- What is the company's free-cash flow yield? Is this a relevant metric given the stage the company is in? How does it compare to similar companies?

- Is the company growing faster or more slowly than other companies with similar multiples?

- Based on the number alone, does the company seem to have a rich valuation or a cheap valuation? Why might this be the case?

Financials

- What has been the trajectory of revenue growth over the past ten years? Why? What is it expected to do in the future?

- How has the company's industry been growing? Is the company gaining or losing share in its industry?

- What is the company's level of profit margins? How does it compare to other companies in its industry?

- How have margins varied over the past ten years? Why?

- What percentage of the company's costs are fixed costs versus variable costs?

- What is the company's historical return on capital? Why is it high/low? What does this say about the quality of the business?

- What is the trend in returns on capital? Why? What does this say about the returns the company will have to make on its future investments?

- What is the company's dividend policy? Why? If they are paying no dividend or a small dividend, is there a danger that the company's management will waste shareholder's money?

Technical

- How have the company's shares performed against the overall market and its industry over the past twelve months?

- What seems to be driving this under/over performance?

- What key news events are likely to impact the stock in the future?

- Do mutual funds and other large institutional investors seem to be buying or selling the shares?

Sentiment and Expectations

- What are the consensus earnings estimates for the next quarter and year? Do they seem aggressive or conservative?

- Does consensus opinion seem overly bullish or bearish about the company's future prospects?

- What insight do you have that the market might be missing that will cause the shares to appreciate?

10.2. Mindset, Resiliency, Ambition

No matter how good your trading record is, there will be times when the market shreds you to pieces. There will be times when you feel completely dazed and wonder "should I quit?"

But that's exactly how this game works. The lower your troughs, the higher your peaks. Many of the world's greatest traders such as Paul Tudor Jones have lost vast amounts of money only to bounce back stronger than ever.

Trading is like life in general—you have to persevere. Have faith. Have faith in a brighter tomorrow. Have faith that when the clouds dissipate, the sun will shine all the clearer. Remember exactly why you want to trade.

1 - Trading gives you freedom and independence. Anyone who works hard can and will succeed.

2 - No one can tell you what to do. You alone are responsible for your choices.

3 - Trading is the ultimate path to wealth.

4 - Trading is the one activity in which success comes in all shapes and forms. There's no single, definitive way to make a fortune. There is no "my way or the highway" strategy. Everyone can succeed, they just need to find a strategy that suits them personally.

5 - Your potential success is unlimited.

Before you use any strategy, consider whether the trading strategy works for you. For example, some successful traders don't average in their trades because they think that doing so only magnifies their losses. Other successful traders believe otherwise, buying as the market does and making a large profit in doing so.

How do you identify whether a strategy, method, or idea works for you? It must two 2 things:

1 - Your personality and human nature.

2 - Your resources (time, human, etc.)

Regarding the predictions, these are simply what we see *at that moment* in time. These predictions change all the time, and many of them are wrong (so don't take them at face value—they are used simply for the purpose of explaining trading techniques). A good trader is often wrong 60% of the time but can quickly correct his mistakes and still make a profit because he is flexible and adaptable.

10.3. Thoughts on Trading Strategy Application

The greatest trades are the ones that occur when three things align:

1 - Fundamentals. Fundamentals include two things: the macro-fundamentals of the economy and seasonal influence ("sell in May and go away," year-end rally, etc.).

2 - Technicals. Technicals include price action, technical indicators, and chart patterns.

3 - Policy. Obviously, policy is only going to align with fundamentals and technicals on bullish trades.

Policy sometimes becomes useless because the Fed can do nothing more. When this is the case, as it was in 2013, you can discount policy all together. In this case, the greatest trades happen when fundamentals and technicals align.

There are many situations in which the fundamentals and technicals conflict. What do you do in such situations?

1 - If the fundamentals are very strong (they all point in one direction), it is wise to trade with a bullish bias, because an economy cannot outrun its fundamentals in the long run.

2 - If the fundamentals are mixed (some are bullish while others are bearish), you can trade on the technicals rather than the fundamentals.

Do what works for you. Any trading strategy is worthy as long as it is profitable. Keep using your current trading model until it stops working.

This doesn't mean you shouldn't improve your trading model when it's yielding profits. Test new improvements to your trading model with a small amount of money. As the new trading model continues to prove itself, give it greater and greater sums of money to trade.

10.4. Tips from the Battled & Scarred

Here are a few miscellaneous thoughts to consider as you go forward and gain some experience. These are not hard-and-fast, black-and-white rules, but nuggets of wisdom that you will find apply to your trading in different contexts.

Some traders say you should weigh all your technical indicators equally, because "by doing so, you'll be very selective about which indicators you use."

Not all indicators are of equal value, even if they're valuable enough to be included in your model.

Weigh each indicator based on how useful it has been recently. For example, if RSI is constantly in the overbought area, decrease the weight of RSI in your trading model. If VIX is sending out trading signals that have been wrong recently, decrease the weight of VIX in your trading model.

***

Some people trade counter to the cyclical market—when they know, for example, that the prevailing trend is downward but a correction is almost a certainty (massively oversold, major support), they will put on a long position, make some money, and get out real soon.

In the beginning, avoid counter-trend trading because:

1 – You are not as skilled as these traders.

2 - Trading counter to the trend is an extremely nerve-racking, hit-and-miss approach because you know the market will resume its trend sooner or later.

3 - Timing is critical: if you hold on for even a little too long, the trend will kill your portfolio.

4 - Above all, there may not be a correction at the price level you went long/short on. If the correction doesn't materialize at the exact time you need it to, the trend will wipe you out.

***

Some successful traders choose not to use a stop loss. Jim Rogers waits until his initial conviction is wrong and then waits for a better opportunity to get rid of his position (thereby limiting his losses).

Keep in mind that Rogers is a fundamentalist, and his stop losses are mostly a matter of personal preference.

Most fundamental traders set up their stop losses at pain thresholds, which is wrong. What happens if the market falls 10%, hits their loss, and then comes roaring back? They lose out.

If your trade is supported by fundamentals, place your stop loss by deciding where the market has to go for your market view to be wrong. If your trade is purely based on technicals, setting a close stop loss based on, for instance, a 7% decline is OK.

***

Scaling out of a position in a bubble is preferable because it's profitable and emotionally and mentally safe.

Great traders have made serious mistakes because they sold out too early. Julian Robertson got out of the tech bubble in 1999, a year before its peak. Unable to stand the pain of not being in the market, he bought at the peak of the bubble. In a bubble, there are two things you shouldn't do:

228

1 - Close your entire long position. Who's to say when the market will burst? We know it will burst, we just don't know when. NASDAQ in 2000 could have peaked at 8,000 just as easily as it did at 5,000. Markets in a bubble are crazed because investors no longer think rationally. Thus, it is best to take some profits on the way up, but if the market continues going up, you'll find it easier to control your emotions because you know you're still banking profits along the way.

2 - Hold your entire position until the market bursts. The only traders who can do this are the true believers. They overstay their welcome, and when the bubble bursts they'll be broke and/or unemployed.

***

The bottom of a market correction has a distinctive feel to it. Only traders who stare at the changing market price can feel this. In a correction, the market falls in 3 waves:

1 - Wave 1: The market starts to panic, but by the time the market makes a small rebound, it feels as if the panic hasn't been fully released yet.

2 - Wave 2: The market continues to panic, but you still feel as if the panic isn't full-throttle. This second decline falls in a very organized, staircase-like fashion.

3 - Wave 3: Between the 2nd and 3rd waves of decline there is a rebound that holds very well at first. All of a sudden, however, the market will tank, thereby releasing all the panic it hasn't released yet.

The third wave's duration is very short, usually only one or two days.

4 - After the third wave, the market's correction is over and ready to resume its upward trend. At the bottom of the correction, sentiment (used as a contrarian indicator) is extremely low—a bullish signal.

***

Some very successful traders do not use stop losses. Here's how they do it. Let's use an example.

The market is falling, but you think it will soon bottom out. By looking at similar historical examples, you see that even if that market hasn't hit bottom already, the market can only fall 2% more. What you do is buy a third of your portfolio into the market right now, and for every 1% the market falls, buy another third of your portfolio into the market.

If the market falls further than the range you predicted (2%), go back to history to see when such an event has happened before. Compare the fundamentals between right now and back then. Are they similar? For example, if you predicted that the market would fall a maximum of 2% more but the market falls another 8%, which is what happened in 2009, compare the fundamentals between right now and the 2009 bottom. Are they similar? If not (because 2009 had the heavy weight of the massive bear market and tanking economy compared to right now when these fundamentals do not exist), this is probably just an anomaly and you don't have to cut your losses.

If the fundamentals are the same (e.g., today's fundamentals and 1987's), then see where the market bounced back to when it stopped falling (in 1987). Will the market bounce back further than where you opened your position? If so, you don't have to use a stop loss because there is a margin of safety.

Essentially, the margin of safety is "based on historical analysis, even if the market continues to fall I can still put in a buy order right now because I know that the market will bounce beyond the price I bought it at."

That said, a change in the fundamentals of a company can act as a stop loss in and of itself. In the 1990s, Warren Buffett had a huge position in Disney but then saw its CEO, Michael Eisner, moving the company away from its core business (animation, family-oriented entertainment, etc.), which raised numerous red flags that caused Buffett to get out.

Later, Buffett was being interviewed and was asked why he left Disney. He replied, "I didn't leave Disney, they left me."

Early on, Buffett identified Disney's durable competitive advantage as lying in the realm of family-oriented entertainment geared toward children, and when Eisner started chipping away at that advantage, Buffett saw the signs of change that would eventually impact Disney's earnings.

If you buy a stock with strong fundamentals and a large margin of safety but don't use conventional stops, you have to watch for signs that could negatively impact your investment's fundamentals and use them as a gauge to scale out.

***

If I had to pick one fundamental trading rule to share with you, it would be cutting your losses short.

Successful trading is a paradox in which you want to stick with your winners and be slow to sell them while remaining nimble and fast-acting in eliminating a losing trade. Unfortunately, people are wired to do the opposite.

It is critical to your success to develop the ability to quickly eliminate losses early on. If you don't, a small loss can quickly develop into a larger one.

The overall impact to your trading is devastating, especially to your confidence. An unnecessary loss can be send you on a downward spiral that can eat away at the most important asset you have next to your trading capital—your confidence.

A confident trader is a force to be reckoned with, as long as the confidence is balanced with strong discipline and the right tools.

Confidence allows you to shrug off a losing position and move to the next trade with focus and detachment.

If you lose your confidence due to an inability to cut a small loss and move on to the next opportunity without churning the memory of that loss over and over again in your head, you're likely to come out the other side a winner.

If not, you can sustain a huge drawdown that can become a deep pit you have to dig yourself out of. A 50% drawdown takes a 100% return just to get back to breaking even.

Resolve now to develop the ability to cut your losing positions quickly and just say "Next!" This will become a mental anchor that will help you move on to your next trade and put the past where it belongs without eating away at your self-esteem or your capital.

Good trading.

11. Putting It All Together

Here, you're going to see how all of the tools detailed up this point come together to help uncover opportunities in the market.

Whether you trade Forex, stocks, futures, or currencies, the study of price action is fundamentally the same. You look for underlying instruments that have characteristics that match your trading philosophy/method and then use a series of technical analysis tools and indicators to spot low-risk setups to trade.

In the stock market, stocks that have strong fundamentals also tend to have compelling technical criteria. Why? Because no security can outrun its fundamentals. Are there stocks that have strong price trends and technical criteria without strong fundamentals? Sure. But as a whole, you want to minimize your risk by selecting stocks that have compelling fundamentals because they have lasting power.

Now, can you trade high-flying stocks with the methods outlined in this book? Yes, absolutely. I do it all the time. But I am also aware of the risks, and so should you be.

Like any other security, stocks cannot outrun their fundamentals forever, and when the tipping point is reached, you better have an exit strategy or a plan to minimize the risks, because they can "flash crash" with frightening speed.

Like a boxer who has been caught flat-footed by an unexpected blow, traders have been knocked out by such surprise moves in the market. If you understand good defense and plan ahead, however, you can avoid the negative impact these sharp reversals can have on your capital. Moreover, if you have a sound method and develop the skill, you'll see them as highly profitable opportunities that are missed by average traders who are too scared to act.

That said, in the following examples you're going to go through a series of detailed trades as the different methods uncover the opportunities they presented at the time.

The goal is to gain insight into how to approach a potential trade and size up the chart's price action to discover new opportunities.

236

As you go through these examples, or, for that matter, how you approach the market in general, be mindful of risk and maintaining a sense of "active patience."

As mentioned in the previous chapter, you never want to approach trading with reckless abandon because it leads to unnecessary losses. Worse, you lose precious time trying to recover those losses instead of increasing your trade equity on future winners.

"Active patience" is coming from a place of detachment where you're observing what unfolds with no mental/emotional energy invested in the outcome. You can cause yourself a lot of anxiety by becoming emotionally invested on whether a trade will set up or not. This becomes a type of domino effect that can result in a trader acting impulsively by trying to force a trade that isn't there.

It's better to let the market come to you, not the other way around. Let it prove to you that it is worthy of your investment by letting it set up to your standards rather than trying to chase a trade down.

Example 1: Icahn Enterprises (IEP)

Carl Ichan has made a big name for himself as a "greenmailer," someone who buys a stake in a company with the goal of unlocking its value followed by that company's board of directors offering to buy his shares back at a premium so that he will go away.

Along the way, his flagship company, Icahn Enterprises, or IEP, has picked up plum investments from everything from real estate to casinos.

In late 2012, I noticed that IEP was going through a strong period of price contraction (see Figure 1) when price broke higher in early 2013. IEP exploded and doubled in just a couple of months.

Courtesy of FreeStockCharts.com©
Figure 1

Fundamentally, the company's performance was average, which is why I didn't try to buy it on the breakout. But any time you see price accelerate the way IEP did in early 2013, it should get your attention that some actionable event is underway. It doesn't always happen right away, but it's worth putting the stock on your "hit list" of potential trade candidates.

At the $90 level, price stalled and reversed in a Game Change-type setup, but with the strong price action leading up to the stock's run-up, I didn't try to short it but waited to see if anything developed. The pullback was messy—down then up, tested $90 again and failed. But after the retest of the $90 resistance level, the price retraced less than 50% of the preceding run-up, entering another period of price contraction.

This time, the price formed a triangle pattern as it began to firm up and find support.

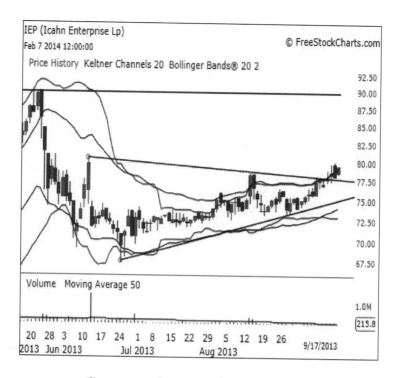

Courtesy of FreeStockCharts.com©
Figure 2

In addition to the Triangle pattern, a Rattlesnake Volatility setup formed as the Bollinger Bands contracted inside the Keltner Channels in mid-2013. These two events triggering at the same time put the odds in your favor that the trade was going to continue trading upwards, and it was time to pull the trigger.

As price traded up through the triangle pattern's upper trend line, you would like to enter somewhere over the previous price high at around $77 to $78.

If you missed that entry, you would look for some type of pullback or long entry setup to occur in the stock's run-up out of this period of contraction.

In Figure 3, you see that IEP was moving up to test the $90 resistance level and pulled back slightly before attempting to break out to higher ground. During that pullback, an inside bar formed on 10-9-2013, indicating that a long setup condition had formed. You would have placed an order ten cents above the inside bar's intraday high at $83.71.

Courtesy of FreeStockCharts.com©

Figure 3

IEP resumed its upward trend, and it would have been advisable to tighten up your stop loss to break even just in case the resistance point held, causing IEP to reverse again. However, IEP traded higher on greater volume followed by strong price action. Strong price action is when the daily price bar closes in the upper range of its intraday trading range. In this case, it gapped higher as it broke above the $90 resistance point.

IEP continued to make higher-highs and higher-lows in stair-step fashion (see Figure 4), pausing occasionally during brief periods of price contraction before continuing its upward move. These brief contraction periods could also have served as new buying opportunities to add to your existing position or, at the least, points to tighten up your stop losses.

Courtesy of FreeStockCharts.com©
Figure 4

IEP traded to almost $150 before falling apart (see Figure 5).

Courtesy of FreeStockCharts.com©
Figure 5

The Game Changer formula would have acted as a framework to guide your decisions on whether to get out or take profits as the stock climbed higher but then declined suddenly. Volume spiked on 12-13-13 to almost 1,000% of its 50-day average, signaling that the move was over.

IEP traded to almost $150 before falling apart (see Figure 5).

The Game Changer formula would have acted as a framework to guide your decisions on whether to get out or take profits as the stock climbed higher but then declined suddenly. Volume spiked on 12-13-13 to almost 1,000% of its 50-day average, signaling that the move was over.

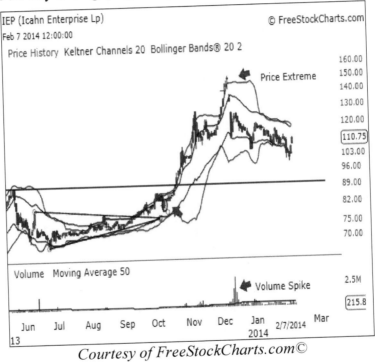

Courtesy of FreeStockCharts.com©

Figure 6

The biggest red flag that a decline was underway would have been when price exceeded the upper limits of its upper Bollinger Band. When price exceeds those limits in volatility, it's like stretching a rubber band to its limit and then releasing it where it will explosively snap back. After a strong run-up of almost sixty points in just three months, give or take, profit-taking at these levels would have been called for, and any remaining positions would have been sold off as volume spiked back in early December of 2013.

There's one more thing to add. If you notice the slope of IEP's bullish run, it is slightly sharper than a standard 45-degree slope. From a technical standpoint, a 45-degree slope for a bullish trend is typically more stable than a trend that exceeds that limit.

Trends that move greater than 45 degrees tend to run up faster with speed that is incredibly profitable. But when they run their course, their end is explosive, and you want to be somewhere else.

The combination of higher trade volume, exceeding the Bollinger Band's upper threshold, and the slant of the trend's slope were all indicators that you should look to exit or, at the very least, lighten your position and tighten up your stop loss points.

Example 2: Core Laboratories (CLB)

Core Laboratories N.V. (CLB) is a stock I've followed through the years and have both traded and invested in. The company provides reservoir description, production enhancement, and reservoir management services to the oil and gas industry worldwide.

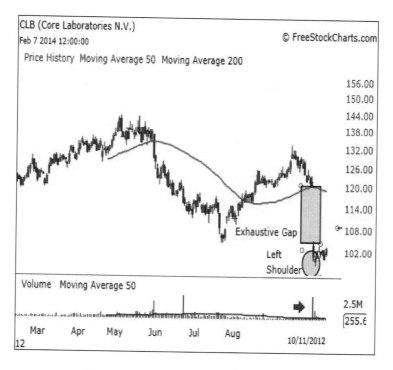

Courtesy of FreeStockCharts.com©
Figure 7

During the housing crisis of 2008, the stock was taken down to new price lows, along with the rest of the stock market. After years of clawing its way back to its previous high of $77.75 in 2007, up from its lows of $24 in 2008, the stock reached new price highs in summer of 2010 and has been steadily making new higher-highs and higher-lows in its price action.

The company is fundamentally solid and has a strong, durable competitive advantage in its marketplace, but in mid-2012 it experienced a price decline. I felt that the stock would recover because it was so fundamentally strong, but I needed some compelling technical signs that the stock would resume its upward trend.

On 10-2-12 (see Figure 7), CLB experienced a surge in volume to almost ten times its fifty-day average, accompanied by a huge price gap.

Gaps this extreme are usually caused by mass fear or hysteria, which have nothing to do with the underlying security. Still, you have to be mindful of risk. While human nature tends to overreact and crush the price of an otherwise good stock, the reality is that you never want to underestimate the other side's fear, which can drive price down even further.

The gap later turned out to be an "exhaustive gap," meaning that all the sellers dove in at the same time to sell and there would be nothing left except those who already held the stock and, later, new buyers.

But for now, as price was unfolding, you wanted to sit back, observe, and patiently wait for signs that the stock would recover.

Courtesy of FreeStockCharts.com©
Figure 8

After CLB hit a new price low on 10-3-12, the stock traded slightly higher and went on to form a lower-high and trade down to $94.72 on 11-9-12, setting a lower-low in its price action.

At first glance, most traders would assume that the stock would continue to trade lower on the side of the bears. In the absence of strong fundamentals, that would be a safe assumption. However, CLB wasn't an unsound company, but a strong company that simply suffered a "flash crash" due to herd behavior, or mass panic.

The fly in the ointment was that the stock's volume was declining, which meant that the sellers might have exhausted themselves as the price gap suggested. Price did go on to make a lower-low (see Figure 8) but lacked the volume the previous price low displayed.

Price did rebound, but it went on to form a steady series of higher-highs and higher-lows until an inverse head & shoulders pattern seemed to be forming. Price also reached the previous high of $108.36 before pulling back and forming the right shoulder of the chart patterns.

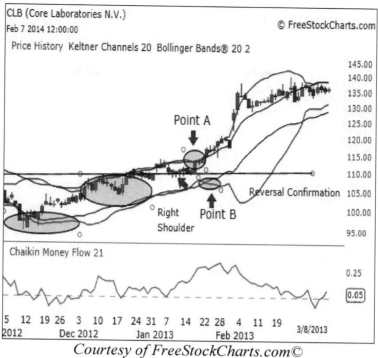

Courtesy of FreeStockCharts.com©

Figure 9

In Figure 9, you can see that at Point A and Point B, the setup condition for the rattlesnake volatility setup was met just as price was trading above the neckline of the inverse head & shoulders pattern. At the same time, the Chaikin indicator traded up through its zero-line and was trending higher, indicating that a bullish move was about to occur.

With a confirmation that a reversal was underway along, all indicators showing that a bullish setup was in place, and with CLB's price action forming higher-highs and higher-lows as well, it would be safe to look at going long in this stock.

On 1-9-13, an inside bar formed during a pullback, and entry triggered ten cents over the intraday high of $110.29 for an entry price of $110.39. The trade was triggered the following day (see Figure 10), and CLB slowly traded higher from that point.

CLB (Core Laboratories N.V.)
Feb 7 2014 12:00:00
© FreeStockCharts.com
Price History Moving Average 50 Moving Average 200

200.00

179.63
170.00
160.00
150.00
140.00
130.00
120.00
113.00
106.00

Reversal Confirmation

Volume Moving Average 50

1.0M
255.6

Jan Feb Mar Apr May Jun Jul Aug
12 2013   10/3/2013

Courtesy of FreeStockCharts.com©

Figure 10

On 2-20-13, further confirmation of a bullish bias in CLB's price action occurred when the fifty-day SMA crossed up through the two-hundred-day SMA. Now, with price trading above its fifty-day SMA and two-hundred-day SMA, CLB was statistically more likely to continue its bullish trend.

In Figure 10, you can see that CLB's price action continued to make a steady series of higher-highs and higher-lows, with the fifty-day SMA serving as support along the way. Each retest of the fifty-day SMA would also have served as a good entry point for new longs or to add to an existing long position.

In July of 2013, CLB began to enter a phase of price contraction during the "summer doldrums," a seasonal period when the stock market tends to have lackluster performance accompanied by low trade volume. After hitting a new high of just over $158 a share on 7-11-13, price pulled back, followed by a strong surge in bearish volume of almost 400% of CLB's fifty-day average on 7-18-13.

Despite a game-changer signal to the downside, price found support but continued to meander back and forth, sending mixed signals as the following price highs and lows formed.

During this time, CLB began to form a triangle pattern as well as meet the condition for another rattlesnake volatility setup (see Figure 11). At Points C and D, CLB's Bollinger bands contracted with its Keltner channels.

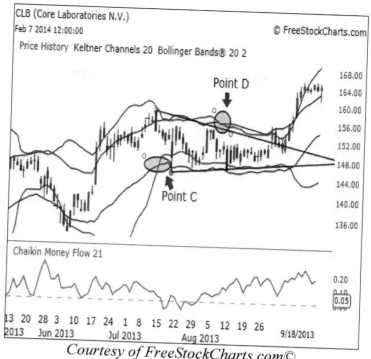

Figure 11

Further support was provided by the 50-day SMA as price contracted on top of the moving average and held its ground (Figure 12).

Volume also stabilized, as seen in the on-balance indicator, which reveals that distribution stalled as CLB went on to trade up through the upper trendline of the chart pattern. The OBV later went on to trend higher, showing that CLB was under accumulation again, further supporting its bullish run.

But the initial breakout on 8-28-13 wasn't accompanied by above average volume, which, to me, showed a lack of conviction on the side of the bulls. I thought it best to avoid a potential false breakout.

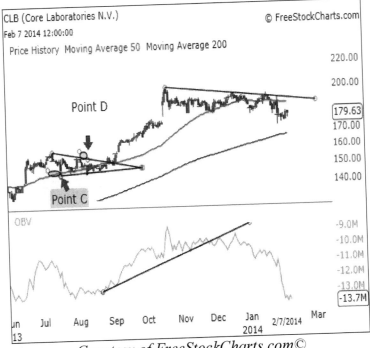

Courtesy of FreeStockCharts.com©
Figure 12

Price pulled back slightly and formed a higher-low out of the chart pattern, and I decided that a long entry above the preceding higher-high, ten cents above its intraday high of $155.50, would be an actionable trade.

The long entry was triggered on 9-5-13, followed by a strong bullish move up to $200.

However, as the move progressed, the angle of the slope of the trend was greater than the 45-degree slope I prefer (see Figure 14), and CLB began to trade parabolically, which is a warning sign in and of itself.

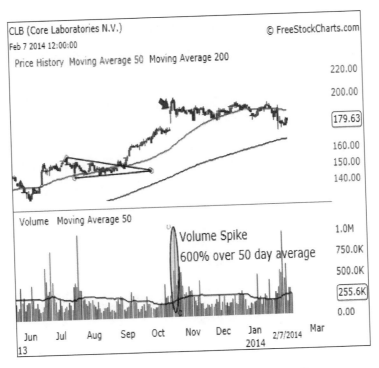

Courtesy of FreeStockCharts.com©
Figure 13

On 10-17-13, CLB experienced a huge spike in volume and traded up through the upper band of its Bollinger Bands. As the stock traded higher over the next two days, I began to sell into the strength of the move while keeping half of my original position. But as the stock went on to form a new series of lower-highs and lower-lows, I decided to throw in the towel and exit.

260

Later on (see Figure 14), at Points D and F, you can see that
CLB entered another rattlesnake volatility setup but that the
Chaikin indicator had become contracted as well, throwing
off mixed signals as CLB drifted lower in price.

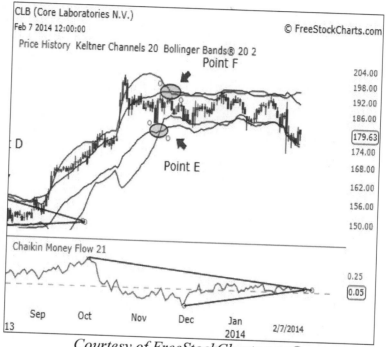

Courtesy of FreeStockCharts.com©
Figure 14

Going forward, I would like to see CLB trade higher,
forming higher-highs and higher-lows while increasing in

volume, before I would consider the stock a good candidate

for trading again.

Example 3: Netflix (NFLX)

Courtesy of FreeStockCharts.com©

Figure 15

NFLX experienced a huge bull run in 2010 as the company gained millions of new subscribers to its online media content. From July of 2010 to July of 2011, from a price low of around $95 to just over $300 a share, the company experienced a gain of over two hundred points, or 200%.

Everything was looking great for the stock until it broke its bullish trendline (see Figure 15) on a surge of higher volume that was a setup for the Game Changer Formula and meant that a price reversal was imminent.

If you had caught the setup in time, you could have entered a short on NFLX as the bears piled on to punish the stock and drive its price down to under $63 a share, a decline of almost 240 points from its previous all-time high.

After the bears wore the stock down, NFLX reached a new price low at Point A (see Figure 16) and then tried to make its way higher. But the bears were waiting at Point B to drive prices back down and keep the stock in decline.

With price rolling over at Point B, you knew the support level was going to be key if NFLX was to have any chance to reverse its course and give control back to the bulls.

Volume was declining, which, at the time, could have meant that the bears were exhausted and had no more strength to push the price lower.

Points A and B were also the first building blocks of a potential double bottom pattern if support would hold. With price and volume moving away from each other at those levels, the odds were on the bulls' side.

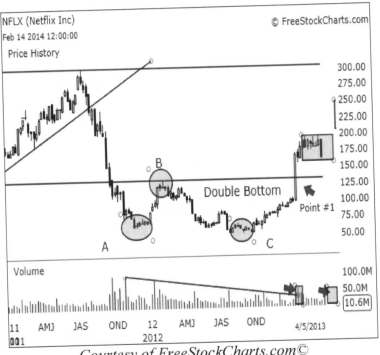

Courtesy of FreeStockCharts.com©
Figure 16

At Point C, price found support and began to trade higher, back to Point C's price level.

At this point, there were two trades to be considered: one, trade off support, or two, trade as price went back up to Point B's price level.

As an aside, trading off support would have been the most lucrative of the two options. Entering at Point B is the most conservative of the two options and probably the wiser choice given that NFLX eventually suffered a steep decline.

If you feel about as to which option to trade, remember that you can always use a combination of the two (which is what I usually do) by taking a smaller position off support to test the waters and add to the position as it reaches Point B of the double bottom pattern.

Point #1 was a confirmed entry at $134 a share as NFLX confirmed that it was reversing its direction on higher trade volume.

NFLX went on to slip in and out of price expansion and contraction, with each phase offering (see Figure 17) an entry or opportunity to add to an existing position (Points #2, #3, and, during a slight pullback, #4).

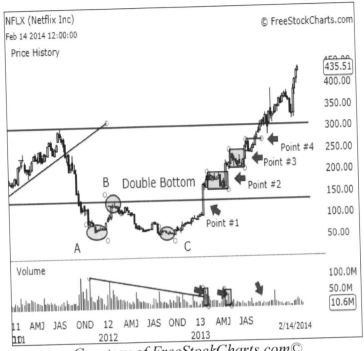

Courtesy of FreeStockCharts.com©

Figure 17

Price eventually reached its former price high of $304.79 in September of 2013, gaining back all the losses it had experienced since its correction in mid-2011. NFLX has gone on to reach a new all-time high of almost $440, and it looks like it will go higher.

From Point C, at a low of $53.05, to its current trading price, NFLX has gained almost 387 points, or 729%, in less than 1½ years.

The Closing Bell

The examples above reveal the potential the stock market holds for traders who come prepared with the right tools and methods.

No one is ever going to catch every trade just right or get out of a trade just in time, but if you arm yourself with a set of rules and maintain the discipline to follow them, you'll be giving yourself a huge edge that can help you succeed in your goals.

Don't expect to be perfect all the time, especially when trading on the stock market.

If you keep striving to improve over time while maintaining "active patience" in gaining the right skills combined with the right tools, you put the odds on your side that you will achieve your goals.

Good luck and good trading.

Made in the USA
Middletown, DE
20 January 2018